School-Smart Parenting

Raising Children for Success and Happiness in School

Michael L. Brock

VANTAGE PRESS
New York

FIRST EDITION

Copyright © 1996 by Michael L. Brock

Published by Vantage Press, Inc.
516 West 34th Street, New York, New York 10001

Manufactured in the United States of America
ISBN: 0-533-12110-8

Library of Congress Catalog Card No.: 96-90616

0 9 8 7 6 5 4 3 2 1

DEDICATION

This is dedicated to Carol, my wife of twenty-seven years, and to Thomas and Jennifer, our grown-up children. May they forgive me for the stories I have told about them.

"What have you learned, Dorothy?"

"Well . . . I think that it wasn't enough just to want to see Uncle Henry and Auntie Em. And that if I ever go looking for my heart's desire again, I won't look any further than my own backyard, because if it isn't there, I never really lost it to begin with . . . Because there's no place like home, there's no place like home, there's no place like home . . . "

-The Wizard of Oz

ACKNOWLEDGMENTS

This book could not have been written without the guidance and inspiration of the following:

• H. Stephen Glenn, whose *Developing Capable People* program introduced me to the world of parenting support

• Jane Nelsen, author of *Positive Discipline* and co-author, with Steve Glenn, of *Raising Self-Reliant Children in a Self-Indulgent World,* who once spoke to our school parents, receiving a standing ovation- they never gave *me* a standing ovation!

• The moms and dads, numbering into the many hundreds, who have participated in my parenting classes and seminars, giving me far more than I could have given them, including many of the stories in this book, especially: Barry Doyle, parent extraordinaire, who introduced me to the Talking Stick; Cheryl Eliason, master teacher, who perfected the art of the class meeting; Sharon Mentesana, teacher-of-the-year, whose television dream has become a staple of my presentations; and Debi Sementelli, world's greatest facilitator, who encouraged me to write the "No-Rescue Contract" for our school families

• The hundreds of teachers that I have worked with over the years- always remember that there are no absolutes in teaching but one: we must never cause a child to lose dignity

• The thousands of students who have crossed my path- I pray that your school memories are mostly positive

• And, most of all, to Carol, for your numerous specific insights in key areas of the book, not to mention your endless proofreading and editing, and for your patience, love, and support throughout- a million thanks! (Next time we go for a walk, I promise not to talk about the book.)

TABLE OF CONTENTS

INTRODUCTION

APRIL IS THE CRUELEST MONTH

April is the cruelest month, breeding
Lilacs out of the dead land, mixing
Memory and desire, stirring
Dull roots with spring rain.

-T.S. Eliot, *The Waste Land*

Thomas Stearnes Eliot, the great American-born English poet, must have been reflecting back on his teaching days when he wrote those opening lines to *The Waste Land*. April is indeed the cruelest month: Ask any teacher. There are a full two months or so before the school year comes to a close, spring fever has awakened any still-dormant hormones, and the students are moving quickly into Summer Standard Time. The roots are dull, the spring rains serve only to frustrate the students' need for outdoor recess, their memory is overloaded, and their desires are focused only on summer. And who could blame them?

The teachers, for their part, are also cruising into Summer Standard Time. It has been a long year, a long year of grading papers, a long year of meeting curriculum objectives that may or may not meet the needs of their students, a long year of working

1

with parents to encourage support for their efforts and those of their children, a long year of working with students who come to them from diverse populations, with needs ranging from basic learning skills to even more basic social skills, and at salaries that are a national embarrassment. And they have long run out of ways to continue to excite students for whom MTV, video games, and the Internet have saturated with wonders and concerns unimaginable just a generation ago.

Yes, April is the cruelest month. For reasons not entirely clear, though certainly related to the above-noted factors, there is something about the spring time, and particularly April, that seems to dislocate families, resulting in a sharp upward rise in the dysfunction curve, a rise that only settles once again when summer brings its welcome respite. At least it settles down for educators; parents may have a different perspective on the summer!

It was an April of some five years ago, a seven-day period in that April, that started the chain of events that led to a new direction in my life, one that has led me from the primary role of child educator to that of parent educator. It is a journey that began with the recognition that American schools will successfully meet the needs of our students if and only if they address the needs of our parents. It is a journey that I resisted at first- I got into this business to help *children,* I argued, not their parents!-, but one that, the first tentative steps having been taken, has been filled with wonders, challenges, and remarkable changes.

For all my years in the "real world," the world of work, I have been an educator. And for the past twenty, I have been an elementary school principal. I don't know what the word 'principal' conjures up for you, whether it brings forth pleasant or not-so-pleasant memories, but it does matter. I often meet parents who refer to "being sent to the principal's office," suggesting experiences that they would rather forget. I hope that was not your experience. More importantly, I hope that is not your child's experience. Today, more than ever before, the principal's office, and every teacher's classroom, must be places of comfort for our children, places where they experience opportunities for contribution, a sense of affirmation, and an environment characterized by emotional stability. Places where they are not "sent," but where they are instead invited and welcomed.

The noun 'principal' derives from its adjective form: I am the *principal,* that is to say the *main, chief,* or *head*, teacher of the school. As the head teacher of the school, I am called upon to be a role model, not only of my teaching abilities, but of enthusiasm, optimism, and positive expectations as well. Mostly, I am called upon to be a role model of positive expectations.

But seven days in April several years back provided a challenge to my ability to enthusiastically project those positive expectations, and I found myself declining into a very uncharacteristic pessimism. Having always tried to live, or at least preach, the old adage that inconveniences are adventures wrongly considered, I found myself questioning whether some recent 'adventures' that were coming my way were worth the inconvenience. I found myself confronted head on with the challenge that education of our children intrinsically included education of their parents, and that as principal it fell to me to make sure that it was done . . . and, frankly, I wasn't all too excited about the prospects.

It all started rather uneventfully. One of our school parents had dropped by to tell me that she was leaving her husband of ten years due to continuing emotional abuse. The stress was proving too much for her third grade child, Maria, and would I take the time to check up on her throughout the day to make sure she was handling it OK? Hardly an unusual situation; in fact, one that I've become very much accustomed to through the years as the divorce rate continues to affect more and more American families, as many as one out of three (and with predictions as high as *two* out of three that a marriage that takes place in 1990 will end in divorce).

But no sooner had I returned to my office from checking on Maria when another mom stopped by. Her husband of twenty years had recently walked out, leaving her with six children and a part-time job, and one of their children, Richard, a sixteen-year-old graduate of our school who was taking the divorce harder than the others, had run away from home. We have always encouraged our graduates to stop by whenever they wish, and many do, often just to find someone to talk to. If Richard should come by the school, she asked, would I tell him that she was worried and would he please call home?

A few days later, I was visited by two of our middle school teachers. By necessity, all middle school teachers are counselors, whether they are formally trained as such or not. Students in the middle school grades- in most schools, grades six through eight, encompassing ages eleven through fifteen- demand a very special kind of teacher, one that can be firm yet approachable, thick-skinned yet deeply sensitive, open-minded yet firmly principle-centered. They must, above all, be good listeners . . . and resist the temptation at all times to sermonize.

These two teachers, the leaders of our middle school, came to me with a concern. It appeared that one of our seventh grade boys

4

would not leave one of his female classmates alone. He insisted on writing her suggestive notes, calling her at home, following her around throughout the day, jockeying for position to sit next to her at every opportunity. It was not long before unwelcome physical contact was being made.

The female student continued to make it clear that his advances were not welcome or appropriate, as did the teachers, but it continued and, in fact, was escalating. They feared it was more than just teenage infatuation, and that it could easily lead to much worse. 'Harassment' was not too strong a word; 'stalking' was being mentioned as descriptive of what was happening as well.

Would I speak with the boy, "man to man," they wondered? Should we invite the parents in and urge counseling- for both him and them? If necessary, could we temporarily remove the boy from the school to protect the girl? I chose the less extreme approach and conferenced with the boy, fumbling through the conversation with my amateur counseling techniques, becoming increasingly aware that just as our parents needed more help in their parenting so too did I need more help in my 'principaling.'

Two days later, I was visited by the same teachers. I assumed that they wanted to update me on Teddy, the seventh grader who wouldn't leave the girl of his dreams alone. But, no, another problem had developed. Another of their students, a fourteen-year-old named Joanna, had brought a one hundred dollar bill to school and it had been stolen. They were concerned that classmates were stealing from each other, but they were even more concerned about what Joanna was doing with a hundred dollar bill at school . . . and where she was getting it.

We spent the rest of the school year dealing with the problem of

Joanna and her stolen money. We found out who took it, but that was hardly the end of the matter. As it turned out, two of Joanna's girl friends had grown tired of her coming to school with large sums of money and flaunting it in front of everyone, so they took it from her. The taking of the money turned out to be the lesser of our concerns, for as it developed Joanna had been regularly coming to school with large sums of money all year long. Where was she getting it?

Unfortunately, we were never able to solve the mystery of where Joanna was getting the money. Her parents refused to acknowledge the problem, they would not respond to our efforts to provide counseling, and the school year ran out with Joanna graduating with her secret. In subsequent years, we managed to put together bits and pieces of the mystery, and our worst fears concerning the source of the money loomed more and more possible the more we learned.

Scattered throughout these seven days in April were three calls to my office regarding physical abuse of students in our school. Working with child welfare personnel is nothing new for school principals, but three abuse calls in seven days was a record for me. Three abuse calls, a mom leaving her husband and concerned about her third grader, another mom looking for her runaway son, a seventh grader stalking another student, a stolen $100 and the greater issue of where a fourteen-year-old girl was getting such large sums of money on a regular basis- all within seven days in the sheltered environment of a small, highly-acclaimed, suburban elementary school in the Dallas, Texas, area.

In each of these situations there was a common element- a parental problem resulting in a student problem. Maria, the little third grader, was having difficulty at school because her mom had just left her husband. Richard, the sixteen-year-old who had run away from home, couldn't handle his father's desertion of his mom. Teddy couldn't deal with his attraction to the young girl because he had no role models for appropriate displays of affection at home- his parents' relationship was characterized by almost continuous hostility and aggressiveness, both verbal and physical. Joanna was raised in a home with parents who held nothing but the very highest expectations for their children's success, with no excuses for not being number one in all endeavors. Realizing early on that she could not be number one in any of the accepted avenues of student achievement- she had an older sister who had already claimed that star in the family constellation-, Joanna looked for other avenues to prove her abilities, and in her confused attempts to attain personal significance found it in crime. And the three abuse cases were all directly parent related. Seven students in seven days seriously suffering at school because of parental problems at home and seriously lacking in whatever skills would have enabled them to bounce back from their unpleasant home situations: Perhaps I needed to take a new approach to helping our students, an approach that focused first on the needs of the parents, and only then on the needs of the students. Or better: Perhaps I needed to see the challenge of helping our students as part of a larger challenge, one that recognized those students as being part of a system, an interconnected system consisting of Mom, Dad, brothers, and sisters, a system in which one member's pain affects all other members, a system called the family.

It was some time during those seven days that I encountered my first introduction to the world of parenting support in the form of a

7

brochure that crossed my desk, an invitation to attend something called the Developing Capable People Leadership Training Workshop, designed and led by child and family psychologist H. Stephen Glenn. Skimming the brochure, I read that at the workshop I would learn ways to help reduce family conflicts, encourage the development of healthy self-esteem in young people, and provide opportunities for both young people and their families to build confidence. I read that we would be looking at families in transition and learning how to help young people develop the perceptions of their own capability, significance, and influence over their environment, as well as developing skills in self-discipline, communication, responsibility, and judgment. And I learned that my participation in the workshop would certify me to facilitate a nine-week series of classes designed to teach those same perceptions and skills to the participants.

I mumbled something to the effect that I needed this workshop about a year ago, not now, but going on the old maxim that it's never too late, I signed up for the three-day training program. If I were to stay in this profession, I clearly needed to experience what this workshop had to offer, and, if nothing else, it would provide me three well-deserved, relaxing days away from school. For at least those three days, I could leave the problems of Maria, Richard, Teddy, and Joanna, the deserted moms, and the subjects of the three abuse calls behind me.

By the close of the third day of the workshop, I was experiencing a mixed bag of emotions. More than anything else, I was overwhelmed. And exhausted- three relaxing days it definitely was not!

But I experienced something else from those three days, and that was a feeling of empowerment. As overwhelmed as I was, as unsure as I was about much of what I had experienced, as physically and mentally exhausted as I was, I left that workshop absolutely convinced that here was something that I could bring to my school parents that would answer so many of the concerns that I and they were dealing with. Empowered with this confidence and armed with my new tool box of information, I returned to my school and immediately scheduled the nine-week course that I had been trained to facilitate. I have conducted over twenty courses since.

The experiences that I had that April and the insights that I have gained as a result of my continuing involvement in classes and workshops that promote parenting skills have led me to reflect seriously on the relationship between parenting and success and happiness in school. Those seven days in April presented relatively extreme situations for me to ponder, but throughout those seven days we continued to encounter all the 'small' issues as well, the more mundane challenges that confront educators and parents every day- homework not being done, children not working up to potential, students stressed out trying to meet their own or someone else's expectations, tardiness, classroom disruptions, playground fights, too much work, too little time, etc. Reflecting on those extreme situations as well as the everyday issues, I have found myself asking more and more just what is the connection between effective (and less-than-effective) parenting and success and happiness in school. What are the behaviors that we parents can demonstrate that will most likely transfer to success and happiness in school? What behaviors can we practice at home that will allow our children to arrive at school more willing to contribute to their own learning, more confident in their ability to learn, and free from any emotional baggage that would otherwise impede their learning? What, in short, is the role of the parent in maximizing the child's school experience?

This book is written from the perspective of someone who has seen what can happen when we take a cold, hard look at our attitudes and values, hold them up to the light of dignity and respect, and reflect seriously upon what that light shows us. It is written by an educator who has spent a quarter century working with parents and children in school settings, struggling to build community among the several elements- parents, teachers, students, business communities, church communities, civic communities, and others. And it is written by a parent who wishes he had reflected on these ideas fifteen to twenty years ago when his own children were anticipating their school years!

It is written by a parent, and it is written *for* parents- for the parents of Maria and Richard and Joanna and Teddy, yes, but even more for the parents whose children are *not* experiencing their more extreme difficulties but who might be experiencing the everyday challenges of motivation, organization, and achievement that all students face from time to time. Except in a closing chapter entitled "A Word to Teachers," I am not here interested in what teachers can do to help the students become more successful in their schooling. I am interested here in what we parents can do. Effective people understand that they cannot change others directly; they can only change themselves. But in changing ourselves, we can often provide incentives and opportunities for others to change. Therefore, our focus here will not be on changing American education- a subject addressed at length at policy-making forums from local school boards to the federal government- but on changing ourselves, so that we can create the best possible home environment for our children.

The importance of this issue can not be overstated. As much as we might prefer otherwise, we simply cannot change others directly. We cannot directly change the teachers that will have such a major influence on the lives of our children. We are not going to change our local school system. And we probably can do very little to change the direction of American education, certainly not in the short run.

And, yes, this can be very frustrating, tempting us to fall into what could be called the "if only" syndrome. If only the teacher would be more flexible. If only the school would change its rules. If only the school board would be more open to our concerns. And those reactions are understandable.

But this is reactive thinking. This looks to outside rescue, to solutions outside our circle of influence. The teacher, the school rules, the politics of the local school board are all largely outside our control. We may wish otherwise, but the truth is that we will have little influence on those external factors. And the more we focus on them, the more frustrated we will become.

But although it is frustrating to be faced with circumstances beyond our control in a matter of such importance to us, it can also be very liberating. It can be liberating if we can learn to accept the fact that since the external factors are largely outside our influence, we are then free to focus our energies on what we *can* influence, namely, ourselves, our family stability, our home environment. We do have much influence within our family, and if we focus there, instead of on the external factors, we will be doing the best that we can to maximize the potential for our children to experience success and happiness in school.

So we will focus here not on what we want the teacher to do or the school to do but only on the things *we* can do, with the confidence that if *we* do our part as effectively as possible, then our children will develop the skills necessary to overcome whatever difficulties they might face, including ineffective school situations. There is much in American education that needs to be changed, and it is incumbent upon all of us to recognize that and take whatever opportunities present themselves to work for change. But the real changes, the truly long-lasting changes, will take place in ourselves and in our families when we make the decision to focus our energies there.

This book is divided into three parts. The first, "The Capable Student," will look at the importance of providing opportunities for our children to see themselves as capable, thereby empowering them to have the confidence to make the decisions and choices that will be of benefit to them as they progress through their school years. The inspiration for this first part of the book is H. Stephen Glenn's Developing Capable People program and the "Significant Seven Perceptions and Skills" that serve as the foundation for that program.

Part Two, "Raising Children for Success and Happiness in School," opens with a look at the most important thing that we parents need to understand if we want to maximize the potential for our children to experience success and happiness in school. From there, this second part of the book introduces and develops the three specific behaviors that I have found to increase the potential for success and happiness in school. Briefly, they are:

• Contribution- creating a cooperative learning experience in the home through chores and responsibilities (with a special section on homework),

• Affirmation- showing real interest in our child's world, which goes beyond the usual call for parents to "get involved," instead encouraging parents to get into the child's world, demonstrate respect for his uniqueness, and foster conditions that allow him to develop according to his own talents, and

• Emotional Stability- providing a family oasis in the home, a family environment that is safe, secure, inviting, and conducive to emotional growth.

A final chapter in Part Two will wrap this all up with a look at what might be called the most important rule in parenting, namely, parental role modeling of the desired behaviors.

And Part Three, "Parents and Teachers: Teaming Up for the Sake of Our Children," will look at ways that parents and teachers can get involved, cooperate, support, and encourage one another to ensure that the children have the best potential to develop as capable, significant young people who can positively influence their world.

I have occasionally used the dialogue format to provide practical application for the principles being presented. An objection might be made that the dialogues are not realistic. But that is not the critical point. Rather, it is my hope that through the dialogue the principles might be made more readily apparent, might be fleshed out somewhat. Look beyond the dialogue, then, to the principles that drive it. Try to envision yourself in a similar situation and create

13

your own dialogue based on the principles you have discovered and your own personal application. Make that new dialogue your own. Practice it. Live it, knowing that practice leads to ownership, and ownership leads to commitment.

One final note. Conversation about school almost always leads to conversation about grades, and this, though probably necessary, is unfortunate. In the one room school house of long ago, grades as we know them today were nonexistent. The teacher validated each student's work individually, met with their parents to confirm their progress, and gave written evaluations in the form of narratives that explained specifically how the student was doing. Letter and number grades used to summarize students' progress are a product of an industrialized world of uniform, repeatable processes that lead to uniform, repeatable products, translated to the education of children who are anything but uniform and repeatable. Interestingly, this is a world rapidly fading into memory, being replaced by an increasingly electronic world, the implications for education we have not yet come to grips with.

But that having been said, letter and number grades remain with us, at least for the foreseeable future. So we need to deal with them.

Do grades help or hinder the learning process? Do they define success and happiness in school? Are we to measure our children's progress through their school years solely in terms of the grades they get? Tough questions, and I will do my best to address them . . . or at least dance around them!

Should we define success and happiness in school in terms of grades? I answer emphatically: Perhaps. But then again: Perhaps not. What I *can* say with no hesitation and no waffling is this: To the degree to which we can measure our children's success and happiness in school at all, we should do so in terms of what they have learned . . . about life, about themselves, about others. If a young person completes his school years with the perception of himself as a capable, significant individual who can influence his environment, and who has learned the various skills needed to deal effectively and responsibly with life, then he has achieved success and happiness through his school years. But the question remains: Will his grades necessarily reflect that?

Well, the fact is I really don't know. I have met many students for whom the grades that they received were true indicators of the level of their learning, and, as a result, it could be said with confidence that their grades truly were reflective of their success and happiness in school. They had focused on getting good grades, worked diligently to achieve them, and succeeded, learning the values of persistence, effort, and self-discipline, as well as benefitting from the subjects of their learning, in the process.

But I have met many others who have looked upon the grades they received as at best incidental to their success and happiness, students who instead have focused almost entirely on what they have learned, with little or no reference to their grades, who focused more on what they got *from* their assignments rather than on what they got *on* their assignments. And what they got most from their school years is a love of learning that carries over into their adult lives in the form of excitement about new ideas, openness to new thinking, and a willingness to take on new challenges.

And I have met many students whose fixation on grades all but destroyed their education. They focused solely on the grade attained with little or no concern about the subject to be learned, and they gained from it all neither the affirmation of their efforts nor an excitement about learning.

All of this is intended to serve as an explanation for why we will not be focusing here on how to help our children get better grades. This is not a how-to book. My interest here is, instead, on discovering what things we parents can do to provide a home environment that will best prepare our children for their school years and support them through the many challenges they will encounter. I *do* believe that if we follow the ideas outlined, their grades will be better than they would otherwise be, and, more importantly, will better reflect their learning. But that is because we will have provided the kind of home environment that encourages effort, that affirms uniqueness, and that provides emotional stability, not because we have focused on grades.

So as we begin our journey of discovery in raising children for success and happiness in school, let's look beyond the issue of their grades to the greater issue of how best to encourage and support them as they experience their first opportunity to accomplish things outside the home. How can we best prepare them for those days? What attitudes and values are most conducive to their experiencing success and happiness? What behaviors should they be learning, right now before they even begin their school years? What behaviors should we be reinforcing as they progress through their school years? These are the questions that we will be addressing, and these are the questions we will discover answers to. So let's get to it!

PART ONE

THE CAPABLE STUDENT

The Little Engine That Could summed it all up rather succinctly, if somewhat simplistically: I think I can, I think I can, I think I can. Succinct because there is much to be said for the effect of attitude on outcomes. But simplistic because, after all, there's more to capability than just thinking it: Try thinking your way to outrunning Michael Johnson in the 200 meters.

The fact of the matter is that each of us has a range of capability, and whether or not we test the outer limits of that range depends on a number of factors, not the least of which is attitude. "I think I can" may not be all it takes, but it is an essential ingredient.

So it's very much worth our efforts, as we begin this look at raising children for success and happiness in school, to reflect on this issue of capability. Just what is a capable student? How does the capable student see herself, and what are the skills that she will need to demonstrate as she deals with life, particularly with life in school? In Chapter 1, we will look at the importance of capability and explore both the barriers and the builders to that key perception. And in Chapter 2, we will meet the "significant seven" perceptions and skills essential for developing capable young people, which were identified by child and family psychologist H. Stephen Glenn and which we will apply to parenting for effective schooling. This introduction to the issue of capability will serve us well in our efforts to understand and put into practice the three key parenting behaviors for raising children for success and happiness in school, namely, Contribution, Affirmation, and Emotional Stability, which we will explore in Part Two.

CHAPTER 1

THE IMPORTANCE OF BEING CAPABLE

"I'm not very big but I'll do my best,
and I think I can - I think I can - I think I can."

-The Little Engine That Could

It was just the second or third day of school, and I was standing at my self-appointed spot- out in front of the school entrance welcoming the parents and students as they arrived, all very much excited about the adventure of another school year. A dad and his son, a little first grader, were approaching me, and as they got to within some ten yards or so of the school door, the little boy turned to his dad and said: "Dad, you don't have to walk me in all the way. I know where my classroom is now. Bye."

The dad hesitated, looked at his son with an expression somewhere between confusion and hurt, and then turned to me for direction. Or perhaps rescue. "What have I done wrong?" he seemed to be asking. I quickly affirmed him. "Go on to work," I said. "You've got a real winner there, a very capable young person, anxious to show you that he's got everything in his little world under control, including school." The dad brightened up, thanked me, and went on his way. Truly this man has a winner for a son, a developing capable student.

On the downside, I observed a mom, well into the school year, walk her little first grader into the school building, into the classroom, and up to his desk; unload his backpack; take out his books and pencils and line them up in the order he would need them; help him into his seat; kiss him goodbye between tears; and then, very reluctantly, leave.

She does this out of love. She does this to ensure that her son's school experience will be free from the slightest possible inconvenience. She does this because she thinks it is her job to do so. She probably also does it out of guilt for some real or imagined transgression, or some inherited baggage, from the past.

But what is she teaching him? What messages is he receiving from her over-attentiveness? What is he seeing in the mirror of her eyes?

To the outside, objective observer, it is all very clear- that he is not a capable person. That he cannot handle the simple tasks of unloading his backpack. That he cannot be expected to know how to arrange the materials he will need for the day. That he cannot even find his own way to his desk.

The negative effects of his mother's rescuing and enabling are clear to the boy's teacher, who reports that his response to challenges is far more often than not "I can't." It is clear to his father, who tries to overcompensate by playing the role of the strict, unsympathetic disciplinarian, thereby only reinforcing the child's perception of incapability. (Of course, just who is overcompensating for whom is a subject of intense debate at the home. Mom will argue that her excessive attentiveness is to make up for her husband's strictness. Dad will argue that *someone* needs to draw the line for the boy, and it certainly isn't Mom!) It is clear even to his classmates, who have taken to picking on him for his constant whining. But it is not clear to Mom.

Jane Nelsen, author of *Positive Discipline* and numerous other works, tells an interesting story drawn from her years as a school counselor working with little children and their parents. When a young child, five or six years old, was sent to her for counseling for some disciplinary matter, Jane would inquire of the child who dresses him in the morning. If the answer was Mom or Dad, Jane would immediately call the parents for a conference and attempt to renegotiate that arrangement, in the hope that Mom and Dad would accept the challenge of working with the child and teaching him how to dress himself. Yes, even a five-year-old can dress himself if we take the time to help him organize his world, provide clothes that are easy to put on, and reflect back to him our confidence in his capability. The perception that I am a capable person comes to us in many different ways, and the accomplishment of dressing oneself is a powerful indicator of capability for a five-year-old. The challenge for parents is to avoid doing for a child what he can do for himself-an excellent rule of thumb in developing capable young people.

School-Smart Parenting Tip

Avoid doing for your children what they can do for themselves.

Then, when they enter school, they will be accustomed
to working through their own challenges and will not so
readily become frustrated with the unique challenges that
school will present.

This story that Jane tells always reminds me of Robert, who entered kindergarten some years back and immediately impressed the teacher with his perfectly groomed and manicured appearance. His hair particularly was noticed- picture-book blond, perfectly coifed, not a strand out of place. In appearances, he was the model student.

But it was not long before Robert demonstrated to that same teacher some unexpected negative qualities. His attitude toward the other students was surly and demeaning. He refused to do any work that he feared he could not do perfectly and better than anyone else. Temper tantrums were frequent.

And although these behaviors continued throughout Robert's kindergarten year, and, in fact, well into his later schooling years, his teachers failed or refused to recognize that he was hurting inside. How could a child who looks so well groomed and whose parents obviously care so much about him be having behavioral problems? Maybe it's bad influence from the other children. Maybe he has an undiagnosed illness- allergies, migraines, ADD. Maybe he's just not being challenged . . . or being challenged too much.

But what they all missed was the point that Jane had picked up on so quickly about the kindergartner who needed to be allowed experiences, like dressing himself, that would reflect back to him that he is a capable young person. Robert's problem was simply that- like the kindergartner in Jane's story, he was receiving from his parents the message that he is not a capable person. He couldn't comb his hair they way they thought it should be combed, so they combed it for him. He couldn't dress himself the way they thought he should be dressed, so they dressed him. He couldn't be relied upon to scrub his face and hands and neck to their satisfaction, so they did it for him.

In each case- the little kindergartner in Jane's story, the boy whose mom walks him to his chair each morning, Robert and his perfectly combed hair- the importance of perceiving oneself as capable is being missed by the parents. How important is this perception? The temptation is strong to answer that the importance of seeing oneself as capable is the foundation of all perceptions and skills that a person needs to be able to deal effectively with life. Yes, it is that important.

To see oneself as capable is to see oneself as having the ability to handle tasks and challenges as they come our way. It is the perception that tells us that as we face those daily tasks and challenges we will be able to work through them, falling back on our accumulated skills, improvising as necessary for any undeveloped skills. Zig Ziglar, the prophet of self-actualization for more than one generation of Americans, calls this the power of positive thinking. Stephen Covey, author of *The Seven Habits of Highly Effective People,* introduced the word "proactive" to describe the attitude that encourages us to take the initiative and act in our own behalf. H. Stephen Glenn, the creator of the Developing Capable People program and the inspiration for this book, takes this quite a bit further by identifying the ability to see oneself as capable as fundamental to healthy self-esteem and the development of the skills essential to dealing effectively with life. It is not too far off the mark to say that without this perception, nothing is possible.

The perception that I am a capable person develops as a result of the experiences that I have, combined with my own internal processing of those experiences and/or helpful and supportive feedback from others. During my early attempts to learn how to tie my own shoes, for example, I will be faced with numerous opportunities for feedback on how successful I have been. The feedback may come from my own internal processing of the experience of tripping over the loose laces or running out of my shoes. I may reflect upon those experiences and say to myself, "Well, that didn't work; maybe I need to try a different way to tie them next time."

Or the feedback may come from others. Dr. William Glasser, acclaimed author of *Reality Therapy* and *Schools Without Failure*, has written that children will see in the eyes of the parents and teachers who raise them mirrors in which they discover themselves. If the significant adults in their lives reflect back to them confidence in their capability, an interest in their ideas and adventures, and an appreciation for their ability to affect their world, then they are more likely to develop positive perceptions of their capability, significance, and influence. If we adults can take the time to get down to the child's level, ask her what happened ("My shoe laces keep getting untied."), what caused that to happen ("Maybe they're too loose."), and, finally, what could be done to improve the situation ("Maybe I could double tie them."), then we will be able to reflect back to the child her ability to work through situations, thereby reinforcing her perception of capability. In taking the time to ask these questions, we help young people raise their understanding from the subconscious to the conscious, thereby fortifying what they have learned.

If my experience with tying the shoes is positive, it will add to the previous experiences that I have had through which I figured out a more effective way to do something- catch a ball, ride a bike, dress myself-, and the developing perception that I am a capable person will receive another boost. I will be buoyed up in my developing self-confidence.

But the opposite is also possible. My experiences, or rather, the feedback I receive from my experiences, may indicate to me that I am *not* a capable person. If I trip over my shoe laces and the significant adults in my life belittle me for not knowing what they think I should know, then I may take that experience, add it to other negative experiences I have had, and reinforce the developing perception of myself as inadequate.

Unfortunately, we adults have numerous ways to reflect back to children that they are not capable. Stephen Glenn and Jane Nelsen, in *Raising Self-Reliant Children in a Self-Indulgent World,* refer to these as barriers that undermine self-confidence and trust in young people. These barriers are: assuming, rescuing or explaining, directing, expecting, and using adultisms. As we begin our journey of understanding how to more effectively raise children for success and happiness in school, let's take a look at how these barriers can affect the lives of young people in school-related situations.

THE BARRIERS

Assuming

Assuming is the barrier that says: I know what you are capable of doing and what you are not; I know what you need and what you do not; I will give you credit only for what you have done before, not for what you might want to do differently today, or what you might be capable of learning today.

27

The mom who unpacks her son's book bag every day is assuming that the boy would not be able to succeed at that task without her. She is assuming that because he needed her to walk him to class on the first day of school, he has learned nothing since then and will continue to need her to walk him to class every day. She is assuming that love requires her to constantly be doing things *for* her son, even things he could very well do for himself. Assuming is limited thinking on the part of the parent that can result in limited thinking on the part of the child.

A very dangerous consequence of assuming is labeling. The father who assumes that his son will be as interested in football as he is himself may assume away a world of potential in any number of other areas. As the boy grows older he finds an interest in, say, geology, and asks for a rock collection for his birthday. But Dad doesn't hear him. Working from his own agenda instead of his son's, he gives him a football instead. The father has labeled his son a football player, and the label prevents him from seeing any other potential in the boy. As the boy matures, he starts seeing himself more and more according to his father's label, and school, which might have become the means through which his earlier interest in geology would be nurtured, becomes instead the place where one plays football.

Assuming is unfortunately a very natural reaction. It is natural to assume our children's needs in terms of what they needed yesterday . . . or a year ago. It is natural to assume that our children will be interested in the same things we are interested in, and nothing else. It is natural to assume that we know what's best for them. But, though natural, that assuming is very limiting, and growth comes for us, and for our children, when we take the time to question our assumptions, an activity that may well be the beginning of all learning.

Rescuing or Explaining

Rescuing may be the most prevalent barrier in our culture. The mom who runs to school to deliver her child's forgotten homework, the dad who time and again intercedes with the teachers to bail his daughter out of some disciplinary situation she has gotten herself into, the teacher who fails to follow through on a reasonable consequence for behavior . . . all are saying: You are not capable of experiencing and learning from the consequences of your choices; therefore, I must step in and rescue you.

In Chapter 8, "The No-Rescue Contract," we will look at a creative way that many schools around the country are trying to formalize the process of discouraging rescuing. It is a process through which parents and their children are invited to put their signatures to a contract that encourages each, as well as their teachers, to be accountable for their responsibilities, and to avoid stepping in and bailing each other out. It's an example of tough love, played out on the school level.

Rescuing is stepping in and preventing the natural or logical consequences of an action from taking place. Explaining is verbal rescuing. It is the barrier that we adults often set up to prevent young people from experiencing the trauma of having to think and make decisions on their own. The dad who while reviewing his son's report card insists on telling him what he did poorly, why he did it poorly, and what he needs to do next time to correct it- instead of patiently asking those questions, providing guidance as needed-is verbally rescuing him from thinking through the problem himself.

Rescuing is the barrier that prevents young people from experiencing the consequences of their actions. Assuming is the barrier of prejudging that a young person is not capable of succeeding at a given task. Directing, the third barrier, could be described as "assuming with an attitude."

Directing

Do you have friends who part company with their children each morning, sending them off for eight hours away from their family, away from those who love them and care for them more than anyone else in the world, with words such as these: "Now don't forget to button your coat, and be nice to your sister on the school bus, and remember to eat the vegetables I packed for you, and don't forget when you get home you've got your chores to do . . . "? Is it any wonder our children tune us out?

Do you know people who insist on determining where, when, and under what conditions their children will do their homework, rather than working with them to determine their most preferred place, their more preferred time, and their own preferred learning environment? Or who sit side by side with their children, directing them on how to complete every part of their homework?

Do you know parents who insist on answering *for* their children, telling them what to say, when to say it, and how to say it? Is the following dialogue familiar to you?

Neighbor: "Hi, honey, what's your name?"
Mom: "Say 'Stacie'."

Stacie: (mumbling) "Stacie."

Neighbor: "And how old are you, Stacie?"

Mom: "Say 'four'."

Stacie: (barely audible) "Four."

Neighbor: "And is that a new dress you're wearing?"

Mom: "Say 'Yes, mommy picked it out for me yesterday'."

Stacie: (completely inaudible now) "Yes, mommy picked it out for me yesterday."

Mom: "Speak up, dear, and answer the nice lady's questions."

Stacie: (to herself) "Why should I when you always answer for me?"

Directing may fulfill our own adult need to be in control, our own adult need to ensure that everything is done our way. And, yes, it works . . . in the short run. But in the long run, it produces resentment, resulting in rebellion or retreat, neither of which lead to a positive self-image or the perception of capability.

Expecting

The barrier of expecting is particularly prevalent in school-related situations, due in large part to the high expectations that most American parents hold for their children. And, indeed, study after study has indicated that children do rise or fall to the expectations that others have of them. Glasser's insight that children see in the eyes of the teachers and parents who raise them mirrors in which they discover themselves is one more articulation of this truth. If we reflect back to young people that they are inadequate, they are tempted to live out that inadequacy. If we reflect back to them our high expectation for their success, they will live that out instead. As Henry Ford said, if you think you can, or if you think you can't, you're right.

But there is a danger, and this is what we call the barrier of expecting. It is the expectation that what we hope our children to accomplish in the long run be the standard by which we judge them today.

I once observed a teacher conduct a forty-five-minute math class with thirty-five eighth graders during which not a sound was made by the students, not so much as a whisper spoken, not a break made in the pervading silence of the room. Never had I observed a group of fourteen-year-olds so on task and so attuned to their responsibilities, and I was genuinely impressed.

At the close of the class, I asked the teacher what her secret for classroom management and discipline was, and her response will never be forgotten: "Not one of these students will ever receive from me the highest allowable grade for conduct. That is reserved for sainthood. None of them will ever reach the standard I set for them. But they're too scared to strive for anything less!"

This teacher had set her expectations so impossibly high that no one could meet them. It reminds one of Mark Twain's commentary about the preacher who, in a blistering hell-fire-and-damnation sermon, succeeded in reducing the number of the elect to a figure so small it was hardly worth the saving.

This teacher had reduced the number of students who in her eyes were behaving at an exemplary level to zero. To follow her logic here is interesting: I expect nothing but the most perfect discipline in my classroom; but being flawed individuals, none of us is capable of perfection on this earth; therefore, no student of mine will ever be recognized as worthy of the highest allowable conduct grade. A frightening example of the barrier of expecting played out to absurd lengths.

Ah, but it worked! The kids were so well behaved! So on task! So absorbed in their work! Yes, to the superficial observer (such as myself at the time), it did work. But beneath the surface, what the trained observer would have noticed was a classroom of students with one goal on their minds: How can I get through this class without being called on or forced to participate? How can I last these forty-five minutes without being seen? How can I make myself inconspicuous? How can I survive this with my self-esteem intact?

There are two roads for a young person to take when confronted by a teacher such as the one described here: rebellion or retreat. These particular students were too terrified, or conditioned, to rebel; the only road was retreat.

But did they learn math? Well, they learned enough to keep the teacher away from them! But only that much. They learned not to question, not to try different paths, not to collaborate with others, and not to make intelligent guesses, lest they draw attention to themselves. To question, to try different paths, to collaborate with others, and to make intelligent guesses- sounds like a good part of the essence of math processing, all lost on a generation of students.

But they were so well behaved! Again, on the surface it appeared so. But what the teacher didn't know, or didn't care, was how these same students behaved when she was not around. They were, in fact, the terrors of the school. No other teacher could handle them. Unable to fulfill her expectation of perfection, they took the opposite route and fulfilled the one expectation they could handle, that of being terrors. Once outside of her room, they wreaked havoc on everyone else. And who could blame them?

We all need to hold high expectations for our children, and teachers particularly need to do so, irrespective of what past experience has taught them about the students. But it is critical that this be understood as a process: Yes, we want our third graders to fulfill all the social, emotional, physical, and intellectual growth expected of third graders . . . but by June, not by 9:00 a.m. on the first day of school.

Adultisms

Finally, there is the barrier of adultisms, which could be defined as the language we use when committing the other four barriers. It is the language we use when we communicate to children that they are at fault for not seeing what we see, for not understanding at the same level as do we. "How many times do I have to remind you to make your bed?" "Why can't you understand this math problem? It's obvious!" "Why don't you do as well in school as your older brother?" These are all examples of adultisms.

Once when I was about sixteen years old and knew everything there was to know, I somehow got stuck tutoring a younger sister in math. Being a younger sister, she was, by definition, ignorant. When she failed to understand a particular math problem as quickly as I thought she should, I exploded: "Why can't you understand it? It's obvious!" An uncle who was visiting at the time, a very patient and kindly gentleman, said to me: "Michael, it's obvious to *you*. It's not obvious to Rita. Why don't you let her explain to you what she *does* understand about the problem, and then maybe you can guide her from there?" I don't remember taking his advice- after all, I knew everything then, so why would I need advice?- but his response has stayed with me.

Adultisms are basically 'put-downs.' They are statements that reflect to the other person that he occupies a lower level of the universe than we do, and therefore he is not worthy of the respect we show others. Adultisms are easily recognizable- just ask yourself if you would speak the same way to a friend. If not, it's probably an adultism.

Do we recognize ourselves in these barriers? The bad news is that they come to us so easily. With no effort on our part, and often with no ill intention, the barriers just seem to rear their ugly heads.

But the good news is that so much can be accomplished by simply eliminating them. By simply *not* assuming that my child is inadequate, by *not* rescuing him when he forgets his lunch, by *not* directing his every action, by *not* expecting him to achieve according to my own expectations right now, and by refraining from disrespectful adultisms . . . I can make giant strides toward communicating to him that he is capable. Or at least not communicating to him that he is inadequate.

THE BUILDERS

Checking

But there is better news. For each barrier, I can substitute a builder. Instead of assuming what my son can't do, I can check it out with him first. And that's the first builder- checking.

HELPING OUR CHILDREN SEE
THEMSELVES AS CAPABLE

The Barriers	The Builders
Assuming	Checking
Rescuing/Explaining	Exploring
Directing	Encouraging
Expecting	Celebrating
Using Adultisms	Respecting

The first grader who stopped his dad at the school door and told him he could find his own way to his classroom is the exception. With most children, we need to check things out. Instead of walking the boy into the classroom, the over-indulgent mom could have checked out with her little son what he needs: "Son, usually I walk you into your classroom and unpack your book bag for you. But I've noticed how big you've grown lately, and I thought I might ask you what you'd like for me to do today?"

If he answers "I don't know," she could help him with "Would it be OK with you if I just walked you into the school building today and let you handle it from there? I know you can do it." How much more encouraging that would be than continually assuming that no growth has taken place!

Exploring

Instead of rescuing, I can stand back and allow my child to work through the problem herself, knowing that it will never be safer than it is now for her to make a mistake and learn from it. And if she stumbles, I can be patient and use the experience as a teachable moment. When she calls home because of forgotten homework, I can resist the impulse to run to school and instead stand firm while expressing empathy and understanding: "Honey, I'm sorry you forgot to bring your homework to school, and I appreciate your concern, but you'll need to work through this as best you can. When you get home, if you'd like we can explore together a more effective plan for remembering to bring all your materials to school."

The builder, exploring, allows us to work with our children, helping them to achieve a higher understanding of their experiences by asking them what happened, why it happened that way, and how that information can help them to be more effective the next time. It goes a step beyond just eliminating the rescuing, a positive step in itself, by providing a process of questioning in a supportive, non-judgmental setting: "What happened that caused you to forget your homework?" ("I never got around to organizing my things last night.") "What caused you to neglect to organize your things last night?" ("I just got involved on the phone talking to Annie for too long, and before I knew it it was time for bed.") "Well, what can you do tonight to effectively organize yourself for tomorrow?" ("Decide on a time limit for talking to Annie.")

Encouraging

Like all the barriers, directing is easy to get into the habit of doing and difficult to break. And in struggling to change our behavior pattern of directing it is helpful to remember that significant improvement is possible when we just do nothing instead. If we can just stop, even in mid sentence, and refrain from verbally taking control from our children, we can allow positive changes to occur.

If for his entire elementary school experience I have reminded my son after dinner to do his homework, and then upon his entry to middle school I suddenly decide not to, he will probably turn to me and say, "Dad, you forgot to remind me to do my homework." And I can say, "Son, it's taken me much longer than it should have but I've finally realized that you're a pretty capable guy, and I know you can remember to do your homework on your own. So I've decided to stop pestering you about it every day." Then I am communicating to him that I recognize the growth that has taken place in him and I have confidence that he can remember things on his own.

But I can go even further than this by practicing the builder of encouraging. Encouragement is the proactive approach to communicating confidence and providing opportunities for the child to perceive himself as an asset rather than just an object of my directions or a recipient of my rescuing. I can say to my son (and the beginning of a new school year is a perfect opportunity for this): "Thomas, last year I reminded you every day after dinner that it was time for you to do your homework. This year I'd like to chat with you for a while about your homework and ask you when you most prefer to do it, where you'd like to do it, how you'd like to remind yourself to do it, and any other details you think are important."

How much more encouraging that would be! No, it may not come easily. And, yes, it does take practice. But the payoff is a more capable, self-confident young person who perceives himself as a significant actor in his own growth and development.

Celebrating

How can we build a bridge over the barrier of expecting? If the barrier of expecting leads us to criticize our children for not measuring up today to the standard we have set for their life achievement, then let's take the time to celebrate- that's the builder-each small step they do make toward the accomplishment of their goal. Let's see their life achievement not in terms of a single accomplishment, an accomplishment that they have either met or not met, but as a series of small steps, each one, having been taken, brings the child closer and closer to the goal, and is therefore a step to be celebrated.

In 1987, the United States Department of Labor awarded a $1.3 million grant to the American Society for Training and Development to research training needs and assess current training activities in corporations across the United States. One result of that study was the identification of four key skills discovered to be common to successful learners in universities and in the business world. One of these skills- that of breaking down complex tasks into manageable parts (the other three were asking questions, looking for feedback, and focusing on goals)- adds a teaching dimension to the importance of celebrating each small step taken toward the goal. If we can take the time to celebrate the accomplishment of even a small step, then we not only encourage the learner but help him to internalize one of the four identified keys to successful learning, breaking down large tasks into smaller, more manageable tasks that can be taken one at a time.

If we can help young people to see the benefit of taking the small steps- breaking down the seemingly overwhelming task of getting all the homework done into smaller, more manageable tasks- we can give them the confidence to keep going.

School-Smart Parenting Tip

When working with your children in learning new tasks, encourage them to break things down into smaller, more manageable parts.

And when they confront school problems that at first glance appear to be overpowering- homework assignments, for example- they will be able to fall back on what they learned at home and make those problems more manageable.

Respect

Adultisms are those tired, worn-out put-downs and demeaning expressions that our parents sometimes hurled at us when we were young and that we swore we'd never use against our own children. But we do. And the reason we continue to use them is that we have not consciously identified possible substitutes. Counselors will tell us that in overcoming addiction we have a greater chance of success if we can substitute a healthy alternative to the addiction. To just say no is not enough; a specific alternative to the addictive activity is necessary if we are going to be successful. So too with adultisms.

The specific alternative to adultisms is respectfulness, and just as adultisms could be defined as the language we use when engaging in the other four barriers, so too could respectfulness be defined as the language we demonstrate when using the builders. And a helpful rule of thumb in evaluating the expressions we use is this: Would I speak the same way to a friend? And if not, what expression would I use instead? For example, when my child complains to me about perceived mistreatment, I might be tempted to respond: "That's too bad. No one ever said life is fair." But would I respond that way to an adult friend? More than likely, I would respond with something more suggesting of empathy than of unconcern: "I'm sorry to hear that. I can tell that it is very upsetting to you." Which of the two responses is more respectful? And why are our children not as worthy of respectfulness as are our friends?

The perception that I am a capable person is enhanced when the significant people in my life take the time to work *with* me by checking, exploring, encouraging, celebrating, and respecting, rather than *for* me or *against* me by assuming, rescuing, directing, expecting, and using adultisms. And this is our first step in learning how to raise children for success and happiness in school: To identify any barriers we may be erecting to their perception of their own capability and to substitute appropriate builders. Our next step is to move beyond the attitudes that we are projecting and look carefully at the perceptions and skills that our children need to possess in order for them to develop into fully capable young people.

The good news is that this next step of identifying what makes for a capable young person has already been done. That work, undertaken by Stephen Glenn beginning in the 1970's and continuing today, has resulted in the identification of seven keys to promoting capable, resourceful young people who can act in their own behalf with responsibility and integrity. These Significant Seven perceptions and skills will help us further develop our understanding of how to raise children for success and happiness in school. So let's take a look at them, and apply them to our own lives.

CHAPTER 2

SEVEN KEYS TO DEVELOPING CAPABLE STUDENTS

"I think I'm making progress!"

-Pablo Casals, responding to a reporter's question about why, at age ninety-five, he still practices the cello six hours a day.

During my college years, I spent my summers cleaning recently vacated apartments, getting them ready for their new residents. One of the 'lifers' there was an older fellow who complained incessantly. The boss was always mistreating him, the government was always conspiring against him, and his wife would never cook his favorite meals. His kids were no good, the weather was insufferable, and these new uniforms they make us wear look ridiculous. He complained interminably about the job, and always had reasons why another person's suggestions for making things better wouldn't work. Life was one long series of things that made his life miserable and were out of his control.

One day I chanced to ask him if he had ever thought about looking for another job, seeing as how he obviously hated this one. "No," he said. "I tried once. I decided to become a fire fighter. But when I sat down to take the test, I read the first question- 'What is

43

atmospheric pressure at sea level?'- and I said to myself, How would *I* know what atmospheric pressure is at sea level? Who *cares* what atmospheric pressure is at sea level? What does that have to do with fighting fires? So I walked out right then . . . and I've been working here ever since."

Well, I don't know how important it is to know about atmospheric pressure at sea level to be a fire fighter, but I couldn't help thinking that the kind of person who quits a test after the very first question would probably be the same person who would drive up to a raging fire and say, "Forget it! That fire's out of control. It's no use even *trying* to stop it. I'm going home."

On the same job I had a friend who was determined to become a police officer, and he was using the money he was earning cleaning apartments to finish college so that he could enhance his chances of being accepted at the police academy. This friend was no scholar, and college was very difficult for him, but his mind was set on completing it and then applying for the police force. During our breaks together, it was all he talked about- getting college behind him and becoming a cop.

Well, he did get the college behind him, but just barely. Four times during the period that I knew him he had to repeat classes that he had failed. He took the classes over at night, on weekends, and even once on weekdays during the summer, negotiating with the apartment boss to come in to work later on class days. And once he even hired a tutor, with his own money, to help him through a particularly difficult statistics class.

Upon graduation, he applied immediately to the police academy. He sailed through the physical and psychological testing, his character review was flawless, but he failed to meet the minimum standard in the academic testing. The academy turned him down.

Undaunted, he went to the library, checked out books on how to pass civil service exams, and embarked on an intensive self-study program. He carried the books around with him wherever he went, studied them every opportunity he got, passed up numerous opportunities for 'happy hour,' reapplied for the police academy exam, took the test, and, this time, passed. He was accepted, went through training, qualified, and is now a detective with a big city police force.

Why is it that some people tend to take experiences and use them as opportunities to learn while others take very similar experiences and use them as excuses to quit? What factors in a person's make-up encourage him to bounce back from negative experiences when another person uses those negative experiences to justify his state in life? Why do some people see life in terms of challenges and opportunities that are largely within their control, while other people see life in terms of problems that other people cause and that are largely outside their control?

It was questions like these that prompted Stephen Glenn some twenty years ago to engage in a study that would result in the identification of three perceptions and four skills that he found to be instrumental in increasing the quality of life in families, schools, and organizations. Studying the factors that were leading young people across America to engage in negative behaviors- declining motivation and achievement in school, dropping out of school, drug and alcohol abuse, promiscuity, gang involvement, etc.,- he developed a profile of both the high risk and the low risk individual. He discovered that the key to determining high or low risk in young people was the presence or absence of the seven perceptions and skills that he was in the process of identifying. He found that young people who are weak in these perceptions and skills are at high risk in the negative areas, and those young people who are strong in them will be more resistant to those pressures. Like physically healthy people who tend to bounce back from illness, those who possessed the identified perceptions and skills demonstrated the ability to bounce back from adversity; those who were missing them did not.

This ability to bounce back from adversity, which we might call resiliency, is as critical to success and happiness in school as it is in all aspects of life. The child who receives an 'F' on a test and proceeds to assess the situation by asking herself what happened, why it turned out that way, and what she can do differently next time is a resilient individual, and odds are that she will do much better on her next test. On the other hand, the child who gets the 'F' and proceeds to blame it on the teacher, or her parents for not helping her, or any number of other external factors is a child who is not bouncing back effectively. As a result, she is more at risk of failing subsequent tests.

These "Significant Seven" perceptions and skills, then, are hallmarks or identifiers of the capable, resilient, low-risk individual. As we review these perceptions and skills in the following pages, ask yourself what behaviors you would like to see yourself practicing and what changes you would like to make in your home to further promote them. In doing so, you will be anticipating the core chapters of this book, which look at Contribution, Affirmation, and Emotional Stability as the foundation for raising children for success and happiness in school.

THE SIGNIFICANT SEVEN PERCEPTIONS
AND SKILLS THAT DESCRIBE
THE CAPABLE STUDENT

1. The Perception of Capability- I am a capable person who can act in my own behalf.

2. The Perception of Significance- I am a significant person who has important things to contribute.

3. The Perception of Having Influence- I can influence my world through the decisions I make.

4. The Intrapersonal Skills- I can learn self-assessment, self-control, and self-discipline and effectively control my actions through them.

5. The Interpersonal Skills- I can communicate, listen, share, empathize, and negotiate with others.

6. The Systemic Skills- I can be flexible with the needs of others, can adapt to different circumstances, and can respond effectively to the varying situations that I will encounter in life.

7. The Judgment Skills- I can make appropriate judgments that are based on firm principles.

THE THREE PERCEPTIONS

I Am Capable

The little boy who expressed his confidence that he could find his way to his classroom on that second or third day of school without his dad's help is a wonderful example of a developing capable young person. I did not get to see him enter the classroom, but I can imagine him walking in, going directly to his seat, getting out the books for his first class, and saying to himself, OK, Mrs. Grady, I'm here to learn whatever you've got to teach; give it to me.

I don't know the boy's parents, but I would guess that they raised him to see himself as a capable person. I would bet that they involved him in the family chores, and that he saw those chores as significant contributions to the family. I can see them affirming him in his uniqueness, listening to him when he talks about his own interests, encouraging him to explore his little world, asking him questions that call for meaningful responses, giving him choices in his daily activities, supporting him when he makes mistakes, and answering his questions. I can imagine a home that is emotionally stable, with rituals and traditions to support the family, and mutual respect as a guiding principle. And I see parents who make as many mistakes as the rest of us but who strive to learn from those mistakes and role model, to the best of their abilities, the behaviors that are most important to them.

If I were to make predictions on that young boy's future schooling, I would see a student with a level of confidence that would allow him to accept each new skill presented to him as one more opportunity to demonstrate his abilities. If he gets stuck, he will focus his efforts, test out other methods, and call upon the support of others. I can see him thriving not only with effective teachers, but with not-so-effective teachers as well, because he has learned that what he accomplishes in life is largely dependent upon his own efforts. I see a young boy who sees himself as a capable student.

So how can we help our children perceive themselves as capable students? First, let's not ever communicate to them that our love for them is in any way affected by their performance in school. Let's not ever communicate to them that our love for them is earned by good grades, nor ever identify them in terms of their grades. It is a terrible mistake for a teacher to refer to a student as a 'B' student or a 'C' student, as if the letter grade somehow defines for all time who they are. There are students who more frequently than not get 'A's, and there are students who more frequently than not get 'D's; but that does not make the former 'A' students or the latter 'D' students. We parents must avoid that trap as well.

Secondly, we must always demonstrate confidence with empathy concerning difficult tasks that they face. We are not helping matters if we respond to our child's difficulty with homework with: "You're in the sixth grade and you can't add fractions! Why, when I was in school we learned addition of fractions in the fourth grade!" But neither is the parent helping who says: "Fractions in the sixth grade! That's terrible! That's much too hard for you! What's wrong with that school?"

The former response is demeaning, leading to poor self-esteem and a lack of confidence. But the latter is likewise demeaning, because it suggests to the child that he is not capable of meeting the school's standards, which also leads to low self-esteem. A more

49

effective approach would be along the lines of the following:

Bobby: "I just can't get this addition of fractions stuff. Mrs. Nichols is too hard. Nobody understands this."

Mom: "Addition of fractions can be difficult. I can understand your frustration. I remember having some problems with it when I was in school, too. What do you think you can do to help yourself understand it?"

Bobby: "Nuthin'. I might as well just forget it and flunk sixth grade."

Mom: "Well, that's one option. But maybe there are others. What would happen if you went to see Mrs. Nichols after school for a little help? Or ask your friend Joey for help?"

Bobby: "I've got a better idea- why don't you just show me how to do it."

Mom: "I'll tell you what. Why don't you show me what you *do* know, and then I'll try to guide you from there."

What is Mom accomplishing here? She is affirming and validating Bobby's feelings. She is communicating empathy. She is helping him think of choices. And she is building on his current knowledge to guide him further.

If she is wise, she will resist the temptation to become his teacher at this point. She will make an effort to understand what Bobby has already learned from the teacher and will guide him accordingly. She might have him go back to his favorite homework place and, after completing a few problems, check one or two, but she must be very careful that Bobby does not become dependent on her checking. Often our children just want to know that we care enough to empathize with their struggle and give them some time. Asking the child what he already knows and supporting that with patience is frequently all that is needed to get him going again on his own.

We communicate to our children that they are capable people when we reflect back to them our confidence that they can succeed at tasks. Homework is one area that we can reflect confidence in our children's abilities, and if we successfully do that, from their earliest school experiences, we will be raising them as confident problem-solvers who can meet life's challenges.

I Am Significant

I once heard a mom, in the depths of frustration, exclaim about her son: "Timmy is a negative cash flow!" Timmy had just recently broken a window in the house, and last week he had lost a brand new overcoat that had cost the family a modest investment. Timmy was indeed a negative cash flow.

Back in 1940 when two out of three American families lived in rural areas, not too many children would be viewed as negative cash flows. All children participated in the daily chores, and those chores were real life activities representing real family needs- gathering the eggs, milking the cows, planting and harvesting the crops, etc. In farm families, every child is very much a positive cash flow.

But today, unless we parents actively engage our children in meaningful chores that contribute to the well being of the family, that is not the case. Viewed strictly from a financial perspective, our children typically add little if anything to the household economy, serving only as debits on the family balance sheet. Of course, it would be reprehensible for parents to see their children solely in terms of their financial benefit to the family. That is not our point here. Our point is more how our children see themselves in relation to the family, not how we see them. Do they see themselves as contributors? Do they see themselves as important members of the family team, with specific things to offer? Do they see themselves as necessary to the wholeness of the family, such that if they were absent they would be missed? Or do they see themselves as negative cash flows?

The second of the significant seven- the perception that I am significant, that I have specific contributions to offer, that I am needed- may well be the greatest human need. The need to be needed- can there be any more critical perception in life than that? Why do gerontologists recommend pets and house plants for their patients who no longer have family members around? Why do successful service organizations take pains to involve each and every member in active service? Why are the simple words "I missed you" such a powerful indication of our love? There is no greater need than to be needed.

This perception that I am a significant, contributing member of the family community also has critical applications in schooling. Homework, particularly, provides opportunities for children to perceive themselves as significant, active participants in their own education. Parents who insist on doing their children's homework (with the mistaken belief that in doing so they will ensure that it is done right, thereby helping their children get better grades, leading to better self-esteem) are only communicating to their children that they do not count in the process of their own education. Their only role is to show up for class and bring the right books home so Mom and Dad can do the right homework. Their own efforts are unnecessary. Their own contributions are irrelevant. They are, in fact, insignificant, passive recipients of their education, rather than active participants in it.

We are learning much in recent years about the importance of cooperative, collaborative learning and its effect on a child's perception of his significance. As parents, we can encourage this in numerous ways at home. Family meetings, chores, family outings, rituals and traditions, games, and other activities that are approached collaboratively can help our children develop a habit of cooperation, which will reinforce their perception of themselves as significant.

I Can Influence What Happens to Me

Tom Peters and Robert Waterman relate a fascinating story in their best-selling book *In Search of Excellence.* A large group of individuals was given a series of pencil and paper tasks involving complex puzzles and proofreading. In the background were loud distracting noises- a mimeograph machine running, several people speaking in foreign languages, someone banging on a typewriter, street noise, etc. Half the group were supplied with a control switch through which they could turn off the distracting noise; the other half were not. As you might guess, the half with the control switch scored significantly higher on the tasks than did the half without the switch.

But here's the kicker: Not one member of the group that had the control switch actually used it. Although they knew that they could use the control switch at any moment to shut out the distracting noise, not one decided to do so. And yet the control switch group scored significantly higher than the group without the switch. It was simply the perception that they were in control of their environment, that they had influence over the situation, that enabled them to focus more carefully and confidently and do a better job.

The third of the Significant Seven, the perception that I can influence what happens to me, is indeed a powerful belief. If I believe that much of what happens to me is within my control, or at least that I can control how I respond to what happens to me, then I will pay closer attention to my options and will be more willing to evaluate alternate choices. If I believe instead that I do not exercise any control over what happens to me, that what happens to me is a just a throw of the dice, then I will conclude that it doesn't matter what options I choose and what choices I make.

I have a friend who frequently says that if it weren't for bad luck he'd have no luck at all. As you might guess, his life is in shambles. When you believe that life is a matter of luck, and that some people get the good luck and succeed and others get the bad luck and do not, then you have a ready prescription for giving up at the first sign of misfortune.

Applications of this in schooling are numerous. If I see myself as having influence over the turn of events in my life, then I will evaluate those events and seek ways to increase the probability of positive outcomes. If I want to get better grades, I have learned that it helps to study harder for the tests. If I want the other students to treat me with kindness, I have learned that it helps to do likewise with them. If I want to avoid detentions or suspensions, I have learned not to disrupt the class. In short, as I gather experiences about school, I learn to reflect on them and make the kinds of decisions that lead to the kinds of results that I prefer, rather than the results I do not care for.

What is the opposite of this perception? It is the third grader who believes that all the other children are picking on him. It is the fifth grader who complains that the tests are all too hard. It is the middle school student who is convinced that she gets in trouble because none of the teachers understand her.

How can we parents help our children with this? To the third grader, we can ask, patiently and respectfully: "What things can you do to get along better with your classmates?" To the fifth grader: "What tricks have you learned to help you study better for the tests?" To the middle school student: "What is one thing you can do to help just one of your teachers understand you better?"

Notice that in each of these cases we are communicating to our children that the solution to their problems lies within them: "What things can *you* do . . . ?", "What tricks have *you* learned . . . ?", "What is one thing *you* can do . . . ?" Follow this up with empathic listening, providing counsel as needed, and steady progress will result. We parents often feel that we must run to school to confront the teacher or principal with the responsibility of solving our children's problems. And there may be times when that is called for. But these should be rare, and only after we have done all that we can to empower our children to do all that *they* can to solve their own problems.

The greatest disservice that we do for our children is communicating to them the perception that everything is someone else's problem rather than their own. You are doing poorly in school because the teacher doesn't like you. You didn't make the team because the coach is prejudiced. Nobody likes you because you're different.

It is so easy to reinforce these perceptions. It is more difficult to communicate that problems are challenges that we believe you are able to take on because you are a capable and significant individual who can influence the events that occur in your life. The key is sincere, empathic listening plus respectfully redirecting the child's thought processes- What can *you* do?- followed, when necessary, by mature counseling. Yes, it can be time-consuming, in the short run. But it pays big dividends in the long run. And our kids are worth it.

The perceptions that I am capable, significant, and able to influence what happens to me are powerful confidence builders that give us the courage to take chances, improvise, and bounce back from failure. Parents who take the time to help their children internalize these perceptions will be going a long way toward ensuring that they will enjoy a successful school experience.

The three perceptions are critical to our children's ability to be proactive in their own problem solving. Add to these perceptions the four skills that build the resources necessary to deal with our many relationships in life and you have created a formidable tool box for success.

THE FOUR SKILLS

The Intrapersonal Skills of Self-assessment, Self-control, and Self-discipline

I have some friends named Bob and Jeri who have been taking

Country and Western dance lessons for some time now, and they commit themselves to taking periodic lessons and going dancing at least twice a month. Front line baby boomers, they are both pushing fifty years old. But there is a big difference between them: While Bob very much looks like he's pushing fifty, Jeri could easily pass for ten years younger.

Their dance instructor is a tall, young, handsome cowboy who can two-step with the best of them. Bob is none of the above. And the dance instructor has taken a liking for Jeri, who is a natural dancer. So whenever he demonstrates a new step, he likes to invite her to be his partner. They dance slow, they dance fast, they dance close, and they dance apart. And Bob gets jealous.

Now don't try to tell Bob that he has no right to get jealous. Don't try to tell him that he is being immature. He will tell you that he is jealous and that he will hold fast to his jealousy and no one will talk him out of it, thank you very much.

But given the feeling of jealousy, which Bob probably has little or no control over, he does have choices regarding how he can respond. Although the jealousy itself might be outside his circle of influence, the choice that he makes in response to that jealousy is very much within his control. He could saunter up to the bar and check out some youngish cowgirl with Louann or Brandy or Betty Sue on the back of her belt and lead her to the dance floor . . . and make a complete fool out of himself. He could invite Mr. Tall, Young, Handsome, Two-Stepper outside for a less-than-friendly discussion . . . and make an even bigger fool out of himself. He could retreat into himself and give Jeri the silent treatment all the way home. Or he can just be thankful that he is married to someone who much younger men find attractive. The choice is his.

If Bob handles the above situation effectively, he will be modeling self-assessment, self-control, and self-discipline. Self-assessment is the ability to accept our feelings uncritically and without apology. Self-control allows us to make responsible choices among appropriate options in response to those feelings. And self-discipline is the ability to recognize that there are wants and there are needs, and that being responsible means taking care of my needs before my wants.

These skills, which are called the *intra*personal skills because they take place *within* us, are used in varying degrees of effectiveness by all of us on a daily basis. When we accept another person's feelings without trying to talk him out of it, we model self-assessment. The parent who responds to a child's fear of the dark with "don't be ridiculous; there's nothing to be afraid of" is telling the child that he has no right to his feelings. A more helpful approach would be along the lines of the following:

Dad: "Son, it's time to turn the lights off and go to sleep."

Robby: "I can't, Dad, I'm afraid of the dark."

Dad: "Well, I can understand that, Robby. I can remember being afraid of the dark myself when I was your age. What things about the dark are you afraid of?"

Robby: "I don't know, Dad. I'm just afraid."

Dad: "OK, what things have you found that help you get to sleep even though you're afraid."

Robby: "I could sleep in your room."

Dad: "Yes, you could, but that wouldn't help you learn how to deal with your own room, would it? And Mommy and Daddy need time to be together at night in their own room. So what else could you do?"

Robby: "If you leave the hall light on it helps."

Dad: "That's a great idea. Let's try that. Also, I'd like to share with you something that helped me when I was your age. If I could hear my parents' voices, then I wouldn't be afraid anymore. Do you think you could try that?"

Robby: "Sure. Now you and Mom go have a conversation so I can hear you and not be afraid!"

What is Dad accomplishing here? First of all, he is demonstrating acceptance of his son's fear. He is not trying to talk him out of his fear, but is instead validating his feelings and communicating empathy. He is modeling self-assessment.

Second, he is modeling problem solving by asking his son what things he has found that help. And he is demonstrating that there are choices, some acceptable and some not-so-acceptable, thereby modeling self-control.

Further, he is sharing with his son some of the wisdom he has accumulated from his own experiences in a helpful and supportive way. And he is giving his son the foundation of self-discipline by helping him internalize the difference between what he might want to do and what he really should do. Valuable gifts to communicate to our children!

The applications of all this in schooling are numerous. One of the most important outcomes of schooling is the development of work habits, the internalization of the basic principle that there are things in life that I must do even if I do not want to. In a perfect world, we could all do whatever we wanted, whenever we wanted to. And a school that attempts to replicate that utopian world by not setting requirements for students is doing a terrible disservice to them, because that world does not exist. The real world, the world that our children will be entering as citizens with responsibilities, is the world of things we want to have and tasks we need to do. The school that purports to teach "the basics" must include, among those basics, opportunities for development in self-discipline. Homework, individual and group projects, book reports, oral reports, independent learning activities, and portfolio development all give our children the opportunity to choose needs over wants. When we parents support their efforts and encourage them to make the more responsible choices, we allow them to grow in self-discipline.

All of this reminds me of Jimmy, a very likable child who, nonetheless, had difficulties with self-control throughout his school experiences. A shove at the locker, a push while in line at the cafeteria, an unkind word, even a careless look could be the occasion for Jimmy to explode in anger and lash out at a classmate. For years we told Jimmy to just control himself, giving little if any help by way of alternate things to do rather than explode. By the time he was in the sixth grade, Jimmy had gained little if anything by way of help with his problems. On top of that, he had matured early and was now the biggest boy in the class, bigger even than his teacher. What would she do if Jimmy exploded and she could not restrain him and calm him down?

Anticipating possible problems that might arise on a scheduled field day, a day of much less structure and much more physical interaction than a regular school day, the teacher sent Jimmy to me with the request that I counsel with him. In past years, in dealing with Jimmy we focused entirely on ways to get him to stop the anger. We told him not to get angry just because a classmate calls him a name. We encouraged him to try to ignore what others might say or do. We told him to walk away from potential conflicts. All to no avail. This time we took a different approach.

Basically, I cut a deal with Jimmy. I asked him if he would be comfortable if the next time that he senses his anger rising to just leave the situation and come to my office to talk. Jimmy has always sought one-on-one adult attention, and our relationship had always been positive, so I felt confident he would give serious consideration to the proposal. I also felt that he might abuse the privilege from time to time because of that same strong desire for one-on-one attention- he might leave a class to avoid an unpleasant assignment, for example- but the risk was certainly worth it.

Jimmy never did abuse the privilege. During the next year, he came to my office maybe four times, each time in the heat of anger, at the very brink of exploding. But each time, as he felt his anger rising, he remembered that he had an alternative- he could withdraw temporarily from the situation, go somewhere else to cool off, and even enjoy that cooling off time chatting about anything and everything with the principal of the school as his anger slowly subsided.

It's been two years now and Jimmy hasn't lost control, or even felt a need to visit my office, since. (Thankfully, although he has not since felt the *need* to come visit me, he does stop by every chance he gets, just to say hello.) What Jimmy learned was the ability to self-assess- "I am feeling angry."- and then self-control- "I have choices I can make when I feel angry, and one of them is to go visit the principal for a friendly chat; I like that choice!" When we stopped asking *why* he got angry and focused instead on what

61

choices he might have *when* he got angry, we allowed Joey to shift from a reactive to a proactive mode, from "I am angry; therefore I hit" to "I am angry; what choices do I now have?"

When we model this at home, we help our children deal more effectively with the many situations they will encounter at school. At home, they have one or two other children to learn to deal with. At school, they will have twenty-five or more. They will encounter a much wider range of feelings and emotions in their classmates than they have at home, and they will experience a wider range of emotions themselves than they had up to this point in their lives. They will meet adults who may or may not be as supportive as their parents have been, who may or may not accept their feelings, who may or may not be willing or able to work with them to choose the most appropriate choices in response to those feelings. They will need to be introduced to those skills before they go to school, and they will need to be introduced to them by us parents. When we model self-assessment, self-control, and self-discipline in our own lives, and work patiently and supportively with our children to help them practice those skills themselves, we give them gifts for a lifetime.

The Interpersonal Skills of Communication, Cooperation, Negotiating, Sharing, Empathizing, and Listening

For years we have started each school day with morning announcements over the intercom, and for years I have invited individual students to join me in making those announcements. I also looked upon this as an opportunity to spend a few quality moments with the students before it was time for the announcements, to get to know them individually, to "get into their quality world."

What a terrible disappointment it was! I would invite them to sit down, and as soon as they appeared to be comfortable I would open with: "Well, how's it going?," or "How was your weekend?," or "What's new?" Their responses were predictable: "Fine." "OK." "Nuthin'."

What's wrong with kids today?, I wondered. Can't they communicate? Aren't we teaching communication skills in this school?

So I decided it was time to put into practice at school some of the same behaviors I was teaching in my parenting classes. I decided to make a conscious effort to ask questions that would more effectively encourage the student to make an intelligent reply. I decided to make the effort to ask questions that could not be answered with a yes, a no, or a grunt. Instead of "How was your weekend?", I would try: "Well, what was the best thing that happened for you over the weekend?" Instead of "What's new?" or "How's it going?", I would switch to: "So, what's the most interesting thing going on for you right now?"

The resultant change was immediate and significant. For some students it was almost traumatic. Their mouths would open, ready to respond with "just fine," and then they would stop, mouths still open, eyes wide, and look to the ceiling, as if for inspiration. I could only guess at what they were thinking: He wants a real answer. He's not going to let me out of here until I respond. I can't get off with "just fine."

Then their eyes would drop and, noting that I continued to wait patiently for an answer, they would respond: "Well, we won our soccer tournament yesterday." "My grandparents are coming to visit." "My mom told us she's going to have a baby." "I passed my spelling test."

For other students, those with highly developed interpersonal skills (a euphemism in the teaching trade for "likes to talk a lot"), my carefully phrased questions opened the floodgates. No trauma here, just the very willing acceptance of the invitation to share feelings. Sometimes I found myself having to cut them off lest the morning announcements never get done! But in either case, real conversation would result. The students would enjoy the opportunity to share something with me that was on their minds, and I would get to know each student better. Not bad outcomes for such a small change.

Try this experiment with your children. Instead of greeting them at the end of the school day with "Did you have a good day?," switch to "What was the best thing that happened today?" Instead of "Did you have fun at school today?," try "What did you do that was fun today?" Instead of "Did you learn anything new today?," try "What is one interesting thing you learned in school today?" or "What did you work on in science today?" (Or even better yet, "Teach me one thing you learned in school today.")

This simple shift in the way we ask questions can make all the difference in the world between receiving nondescript responses or intelligent, thought-out responses. But be patient: Just because *we* make a change does not necessarily mean our children will respond to that change immediately. The first time you ask "What was the best thing that happened to you today?" they may very well respond with "fine." Or they may say nothing, wondering what your hidden agenda is or why you started reading that stupid parenting book! But keep at it. And, most important, sincerely and patiently listen when they *do* respond. And be sure to pick up the conversation from their response, not from your own agenda. In doing so, you will encourage communication and model respect. And your children will become more conscious of what is happening at school when they believe that you are anxious to listen patiently to their thoughts and experiences.

The Systemic Skills of Adaptability, Flexibility, and Responsibility

Are we dads and moms always on the same page when it comes to our expectations for our children? Are our discipline standards always the same? Are our discipline *practices* always the same? Do the very same things annoy both of us, and do we agree all the time on what are the small matters that we can ignore and what are the large matters that demand our attention? Of course not.

The same goes for teachers. Teachers come from a wide variety of backgrounds and experiences, with value systems that may or may not parallel those of the majority of their students. There will be teachers who more often than not are too strict; there will be others who more often than not are too permissive. The very best will approach a level of consistency that varies only occasionally. And the very best schools will practice a philosophy of discipline and standards that all their teachers will buy into and, with few exceptions, practice. But individual differences will always remain, and our students need to be able to accept those differences and adapt to them.

Responsibility, which on the most basic level is simply the ability to choose a more appropriate response from among various options rather than just to react, is the natural outcome of adaptability and flexibility. The more we are able to adapt to different circumstances and demands and the more willing we are to be flexible with different needs, the more proficient we will become at responding to the demands of life effectively.

How can we model this for our children? So much can be accomplished simply by the way we respond to our children's complaints about school, as demonstrated by the following dialogue:

Catherine: "This school is so stupid. The math teacher gives us detentions if we forget to raise our hands, and the social studies teacher lets us do anything we want. Why can't they get their act together?"

Dad: "That can be frustrating. I can remember having teachers like that. It's hard to remember how to act sometimes."

Catherine: "I know. I got a detention from the math teacher and it's the school's fault!"

Dad: "Well, we probably can't change the way your teachers handle discipline, although I can understand why you might want to. So what can you do to avoid getting into trouble in math class again."

Catherine: "Maybe I'll write in huge letters across my math book 'Catherine, you are in math class now. Remember that you're not allowed to breathe for the next 50 minutes!'"

Dad: "Great idea! And on your social studies notebook, why don't you write 'Catherine, breathe the sweet air of freedom!' Let me know how your plan works."

Empathy, a little humor, and a lesson in adaptability- all leading to a more responsible student. Notice that Dad felt no need to criticize his daughter for her negative attitude. No need to pontificate about responsibility. No need to play the role of the authoritarian parent. Just a little empathy. And respect.

Adaptability, flexibility, and responsibility are called the systemic skills because they are essential to effective functioning within the several systems that we find ourselves involved with in life. Schools, families, work places, service organizations, and places of worship are all examples of systems the effective participation in which demands that we adapt to changing conditions, be flexible in responding to various needs, and be responsible regarding our commitments. In the above dialogue, Dad modeled flexibility, adaptability, and responsibility by helping Catherine identify her alternatives, helping her see which alternatives are more effective in which settings, and redirecting accountability back to her in a respectful and nonjudgmental manner. Catherine is much more likely to internalize flexibility, adaptability, and responsibility through Dad's handling of her frustration than she would if he went into lecture mode, telling her what she did wrong, why she did it wrong, and what she needs to do to fix it.

Judgment Skills

The ability to make appropriate judgments is the highest level skill that our young people will need in order to deal effectively and responsibly with life. This seventh of the Significant Seven is really the fruit of the previous six. I will not make effective judgments if I do not believe that I am a capable person who can figure things out on my own, that what I do is of significance, and that what eventually happens to me is a result of the decisions I make. And my judgments will have a much less chance of being appropriate if I lack self-discipline, have weak interpersonal skills, and have failed to learn responsibility. So how can we help our children make more effective, more appropriate, and more ethical judgments that take into account not only their own wants and needs but those of others as well? How can we help them make "good judgments" rather than "poor judgments" in their school experiences?

This question leads us directly into the very sensitive area of classroom behavior. Classroom behavior used to be a very simple affair. If a child acted up, the teacher responded quickly and forcefully. And so too would the parents. (And, not too long ago, so too did the neighbors. If Mrs. Campbell, who lived on the corner and knew everything that was going on in our neighborhood- particularly, so it seemed, what the Brock boys were up to- caught me throwing snow balls at cars on the way home from school, my mother would know about it before I reached home. And she would thank Mrs. Campbell for the information.)

For better or worse, that scenario has changed. It may take a whole village to raise a child, but today's villages have become too fragmented and polarized to rise to that important challenge. And so the issue of classroom behavior has become a more sensitive one, and a more difficult one for today's teachers to deal with. For our part as parents, we need to ask ourselves, frankly and honestly, how do we want our children to behave in the classroom? Do we want them to behave as if the entire world revolves around their every want and need? Do we want them to be class clowns? Do we want them to be disruptive? Or do we, instead, want them to be respectful of others, be those others their classmates or their teachers?

The key to this lies in the word 'respect,' a word that will surface repeatedly throughout our look at how to raise children for success and happiness at school. It is a word that I believe to be fundamental to everything we do in life. It is a word that offers an opening for a solution to much if not all of the world's ills, from the family to the global community. And it is a word that is much misunderstood.

Most of us grew up hearing that we were supposed to respect our elders. Most likely, we were taught that the mother is supposed to respect the father and the children are supposed to respect the parents. If you were in the military, you were taught to respect the higher rank. And all of that is fine, so far as it goes. Unfortunately, it doesn't go very far at all.

Respect is not a one-directional virtue. It is not meant to flow exclusively in a vertical path, from the 'lower' to the 'higher.' Nor is it something that is deserved by the 'higher' and earned by the 'lower.' It is, on the other hand, something that is owed to every human being by virtue of their very humanity. It is owed by the wife to the husband, and it is owed by the husband to the wife. It is owed by the son to the father, and it is owed by the father to the son. And it is owed by one friend to another. In short, respect is not earned; it is owed.

One of the saddest relationships that I have encountered in working with parents and children over the years is what I would call the relationship of rank. Stemming from the parent's inability to understand that the structure of relationships in the military does not translate well to the family, it results in the home environment in which the relationship between the father and the children- and sometimes between the father and the mother- is not one of love but one of rank. The children are taught that the father is someone you respect because he outranks you . . . and probably because you have been taught to fear him. The idea of respect being a correlative of love is non-existent. And there is absolutely no understanding of respect being owed. "You want my respect, you'll have to earn it."

We model respect for our children and we teach them to respect others- *all* others, older and younger, richer and poorer, of every race and belief- when we treat them and others respectfully. It really is that simple. Not easy to do, of course, but simple to understand. When we speak to our children as if they really are persons of dignity, we teach them respect. When our children see us dealing respectfully with all the people we come in contact with- our neighbors, the salesperson at the store, the secretary at the office, the workers who come to our homes- they too will learn that respect. And it will transfer to school, where they will treat their classmates and their teachers with the respect that they too are owed.

School-Smart Parenting Tip

Model respect in all interactions- at home, with the neighbors, out shopping, at sports and other activities. There is no other way to teach respect than to model it.

Our children will then transfer that respectfulness that they have experienced at home to their school interactions- with their classmates, with their teachers, and with other adults.

If we add to this modeling of respectfulness the concerted effort to work with our children in problem solving and decision making, we will further reinforce effective and appropriate judgment skills. If we have role modeled that there are limits to what we should do, if we have taken the time to clarify those limits with our children, if we have allowed choices within those limits, if we have supported our children in making their own choices, if we have allowed them to make poor choices (remembering that it will never be safer for them to make poor choices than it is when they are younger) and then worked with them to evaluate those choices, always looking for solutions rather than blame, then we will go a long way toward helping them learn effective and appropriate judgment skills.

If I can resist telling my son what the most appropriate response to a situation would be, and instead ask him what he thinks he should do, offering assistance as needed from the wisdom I have stored up from my wider range of experiences, then I will be supporting him in his efforts to practice judgment skills. And this will help him in more than his schooling, as he enters a world far more complex than the one his parents entered. We need good judgment makers like never before, and it all starts in the home.

The Significant Seven perceptions and skills, together with the emphasis placed in the previous chapter on removing the barriers to our children's developing perception of themselves as capable young people, provide the essential foundation for Part Two of this book. We are now able to improve on that foundation by enhancing our understanding of the specific parenting behaviors necessary for raising children for success and happiness in school. Our next step will be to identify and explore those behaviors- Contribution,

Affirmation, and Emotional Stability- and make them our own. Our journey of understanding has just barely begun!

PART TWO

RAISING CHILDREN FOR SUCCESS AND
HAPPINESS IN SCHOOL

"So just what is the most important thing I need to be doing to ensure that my child's school years will be happy and successful?"

That question, raised by parents every year as they approach their child's first school experience, takes center stage in this second part of our look at raising children for success and happiness in school. The answer lies in focusing on our parenting and building a home environment characterized by Contribution, Affirmation, and Emotional Stability. But how is that accomplished?

In Chapter 3 we will identify that most important thing we need to do to support our children's education. In Chapters 4, 5, and 6, we will identify and explore ways to create that home environment of Contribution, Affirmation, and Emotional Stability. And in Chapter 7, we will remind ourselves of the importance of walking the talk-role modeling- if we really want to help our children develop into capable students.

CHAPTER 3

THE MOST IMPORTANT THING

"Who am I? I am my kid's mom."

-Dr. Laura Schlessinger

Syndicated talk show host and best-selling author Dr. Laura Schlessinger likes to open her radio show by introducing her engineer, her producer, her call screener, and herself, the last with what has become her signature opening: "And me? I am my kid's mom." Of all the parts that make up Dr. Laura, of all the roles she plays in life, that of being Mom is the one she uses to introduce herself to a national radio audience. "I am my kid's mom."

With that opening, Dr. Laura answers the question that is asked of me frequently during parent conferences and at parenting presentations and workshops: "What is the most important thing we can do to help our child have a successful school experience?" Or: "How can I raise my child to be a capable student?" Or: "What can I do to most effectively support my child's education?" The answer? Just be your kid's mom. Or your kid's dad.

When Joey started school, his dad, a teacher, decided that he would assume the full responsibility for his son's education.

Everything Joey would learn in life would come from Dad. Joey became Dad's little project, through which he could justify his own worthiness to the world.

And so it came to be. Joey brought home his homework, and Dad sat by his side telling him the correct way to do it. When Joey protested that that was not the way the teacher taught him, Dad assured him that he knew best. After all, he was a teacher too.

As Joey progressed through the grades and entered sports, his dad became a coach and decided that he would assume full responsibility for his son's athletic development. Whenever possible, Dad took over the coaching position so that he could direct his son every step of the way. When this was not possible, Dad would reteach Joey, showing him the real way to kick the ball or hold the bat. Again, when Joey protested that that was not the way that the coach had taught him, Dad assured him that he knew best. Was he not, after all, a coach as well?

When Joey reached the third grade, the first signs of discipline problems surfaced. It began with what appeared to be a conscious tuning out of the teachers, an intentional refusal to accept their instruction. Considering what had been occurring for the past four years, this was no surprise: Why pay attention to the teachers at school when Dad is going to explain it all to me when I get home?

But soon the tuning out turned to overt disrespect. This lack of respectfulness was demonstrated not only toward the teachers, but to all other adults as well- cafeteria workers, recess moderators, library personnel, coaches, etc. Dad blamed it on the school: It just wasn't meeting Joey's needs; it just wasn't challenging him enough.

When Joey reached the fifth grade, Dad decided that he needed to be placed in a more challenging school. Joey resented being taken away from all his friends, but, of course, Dad knew best.

Although the new school, a private school for the gifted, was more challenging, Joey's discipline problems only got worse. The disrespect toward adults worsened, and an attitude of disrespect for his peers started to evidence itself as well. He was removed from games by referees, and removed from classrooms by teachers. By the end of the sixth grade, the new school had had enough of Joey. He had to be dismissed.

In desperation, Joey's parents called the principal of the old school and asked if he could be given a new chance there. He was, but he was only able to last a year. Disappointed with his continuing lack of progress and worsening discipline problems, his parents enrolled him in a school for students with motivation problems. It was his third school in three years. And throughout it all, Dad insisted on being Joey's teacher and coach.

Dad had made a terrible mistake, one that, tragically, he would never fully understand. Instead of being a parent to Joey, he became his teacher and coach. Joey didn't need a teacher and coach. He needed a dad. And so he rebelled.

This is an extreme case, but a true one. We parents really have just one role to play regarding our children and that is to be the very best parents we can be. Although we will have plenty of opportunities to support and guide our children in their schooling, we do not need to be their formal classroom instructors. And although we will have numerous opportunities to coach them through the many school challenges they will face, we do not need to assume responsibility for the totality of their athletic development. We just need to be their parents.

The temptation to be more than our kid's mom or our kid's dad is a strong one. Whether it be fear of letting go, guilt for not doing all that we feel we should be doing, distrust of the school system, our own negative school experiences, or whatever, many parents today feel that they need to take a far more active role in their children's education than their own parents took in theirs. And, interestingly, many school personnel have come to believe, in response to societal changes, that the school system should be taking a more active role in the children's lives than just teaching the "three R's," a role that has expanded to touch on areas that in previous generations were reserved for the parents. Continuing public debates over such issues as sex education and values education are actually representative of much larger questions: What is the role of the school system? What is the role of the teacher? And what is the role of the parent?

What is the role of the teacher? One response would be to say that the teacher's role is best defined in terms of the legal expression *in locus parentis.* No, it doesn't have anything to do with the way our children make us feel, or a condition that comes over us after the second or third week of summer. It's Latin for "in the place of the parents," and it suggests that the teacher's role is to take the place of the child's parents during the school day.

But why do we parents need someone else to take our place when it comes to the formal education of our children? Why can't we just take care of that ourselves? Why do we need teachers to do it for us? Is it that we don't have enough time? Is it not a high enough priority for us? Is it lack of expertise? Perhaps. But even if we had the time, the desire, and the expertise, we parents are better off not being our children's formal teachers.

Why not? Isn't it often said that we parents are our children's first teachers? Yes, it is. And yes, we are. But what does that mean? Does it mean that it is primarily the parents' job to be the first to teach the alphabet, the numbers, and how the child should write his name? Does it mean that it is our responsibility as parents to teach long division, the distinctions between the three branches of our government, and the workings of photosynthesis? Or does it mean instead that we parents, by virtue of our very role as parents, will be our children's first teacher in the course of our daily activities together? And there is the key- *in the course of our daily activities together.*

In the course of our daily activities together, we parents do in fact teach. We teach values through our role modeling and through our exhortations. In our interactions with other adults and children-shopping, taking them to our work place, visiting at family and neighborhood gatherings, attending our place of worship-, we teach interpersonal skills. We teach sensitivity, tolerance, patience, self-discipline, empathy and the whole range of emotional responses as we face life's daily challenges with our children. We teach organization skills by encouraging their desire to collect and sort things, by helping them learn how to clean their room and put away their toys, and by giving them chores to do around the house.

We teach correct grammar, again through our role modeling and exhortation. (My mother worked heroically to teach me to say "I saw it" instead of "I seen it," once having me repeat "I saw it" one thousand times. To this day I still take pleasure in getting a rise out of her by saying "I seen it.")

We teach math while cooking, preparing the meals, and setting the dinner table ("Please measure a half cup of milk for me.", "How

81

many knives, forks, and spoons will we need?"), while shopping at the grocery store ("This is a small orange. Pick out three that are larger."), and while doing the bills ("How much will we have left in the account if we buy that soccer ball?").

We teach history and geography while conversing about our own family heritage, and while walking through our neighborhood and traveling around our country. If American history is little more than the study of immigration, as President Kennedy suggested in one of his more famous quotes, then how better could that be explained than through discussions of our own family history of immigration-complete with stories of why our ancestors left (whether it was yesterday or a thousand years ago), why they came to America, where they first settled, where they migrated, and how they contributed? And no classroom lesson on mountains and valleys, cities and countryside, oceans and deserts, or forests and plains could possibly compete with what is learned while driving across America. (Nothing I learned in elementary school about mountains and valleys could possibly prepare me for what I experienced the first time I drove over the Rockies.)

We can open our children to the wonderful world of science just by taking advantage of what we come into contact with on a daily basis. We teach them astronomy and earth science when we talk to them about the sun and the moon, the stars and the planets, the seasons of the year, and the rocks and stones they pick up and climb over and scrape their knees on. We teach them biology when we answer their many questions about the animals and plants they see in the neighborhood or in the zoo. We allow them to discover the basic principles of science on their own if we avoid the temptation to fill their rooms with all the latest toys advertised on television and instead provide them with the rudiments of creative play- empty boxes, blocks and geometric shapes (cubes, spheres, inclined planes, arches, pillars, etc.), string, clay, and paper.

We help our children broaden their horizons, expand their awareness of their world, provide further opportunities for their natural curiosity, and open their minds to a more ready acceptance of what they will be learning in school when we take them to libraries, museums, live performances, parks, historical monuments, and different natural environments. We enhance their cultural literacy (a critical factor in developing reading skills, according to best-selling author E. D. Hirsch) when we read them stories about the men and women, places and events, music and arts, and myths and legends that comprise the American experience.

We teach the names of all the things we encounter in the world. We teach table manners. We teach communication skills. In short, we teach continuously, naturally, and informally- *in the course of our daily activities together.* We teach without a formal classroom, without a standard curriculum, and without any teaching aids. (And, interestingly, without television, "educational toys," or trips to theme parks.) Our teaching flows naturally from our parenting, and the more natural it is, the more successful it will be.

Classroom educators, on the other hand, teach in a very formal setting, with curriculum guides that outline minimum competencies, and in an environment that could be described as quite unnatural. What could be more unnatural than learning in artificial time segments with age as the primary grouping determinant? Do we parents teach manners between, say, 9:30 and 10:15 only? Do you know of any families where all the children are the same age? And there are twenty-five of them?

83

But that is schooling as we know it and, frankly, it appears to be working rather well for the majority of students. In that unnatural setting, teachers very effectively teach spelling, sentence construction, division of fractions, and the causes of the Civil War. Across America, children are learning biology, civics, phonics, and the difference between simile and metaphor, all in those very unnatural settings we call schools. Could it be that some learning does in fact take place more effectively in unnatural, structured settings?

It would appear to be so. Perhaps there is something about the very formality and structure and unnaturalness of school that creates an environment conducive to learning about things the relevance of which is not at the moment clear to the learner. That old complaint about schools not making content relevant to the student may very well be true, but it is besides the point; much of what we learn is irrelevant to our present but critical to our future, or critical to the learning of something else that *is* relevant. And the formality and structure and unnaturalness of schooling make it possible for the learning of those things to take place more effectively than otherwise.

A case in point might be a class lesson on the Bill of Rights. Can you imagine trying to teach the Bill of Rights through the course of your daily parenting? "While you're cutting that apple into four parts, dear, I am reminded of the third amendment proscription against the quartering of soldiers . . . " I don't think so. But we would all agree that our children should be well versed in the cornerstone of our rights, and should achieve a degree of literacy in understanding them so that they could appreciate what we, as soon-to-be twenty-first century Americans, have inherited and what we must preserve. And the formal setting of the classroom appears to be the place most conducive to learning that.

Given all the above, how can we answer our initial question: "What is the best thing we can do to help our children succeed in school?" Again, the answer is both simple and difficult, simple in understanding but difficult in practice: Just be the very best parents we can be. Focus on the naturalness of parenting, not the unnaturalness of formal teaching. Focus on being the very best parents we can be.

School-Smart Parenting Tip

Teach your children through your natural everyday activities with them- at home, at the store, while walking through the neighborhood.

When they enter school they will be better prepared to experience the naturalness and relevance of learning, and more accustomed to apply what they will be learning in the classroom to their own lives.

We parents do not need to be our children's formal classroom teachers. We do not need to explain the differences between islands and peninsulas, vowels and consonants, nouns and verbs (unless, of course, these things come up *naturally* in the course of our daily activities together.)

We do not need to mortgage our homes to purchase all the latest educational toys. Our children will not suffer if we deprive them of ready access to the Internet during their preschool years. In fact, they will gain far more just playing with crayons and cardboard boxes and blocks and lumps of clay.

We do not even need to teach our children to read. Read to your children, yes, but don't worry about *teaching* them to read. Give them your one-on-one attention, your closeness, your warmth, and read them the stories you have come to love. Let them experience your excitement about reading and your love for reading. Let them hear the sound of your voice as it rises and falls, as it expresses fear and joy and sadness and determination, showing a full range of emotions that will enhance your child's emotional growth. Let them develop their imaginations, explore their fantasies, confront their fears, all while nestled safely in your arms. Make reading one of your most nurturing parenting moments. Do it often. Make it a daily ritual. But don't worry about teaching them to read. Teachers will take care of that.

School-Smart Parenting Tip

Read to your children often . . . but don't worry about teaching them to read.

And when they start their school years, they will see reading as a familiar and comfortable experience, one that they have come to associate with nurturing, warmth, personal attention, and positive family experiences.

And as our children progress through their school years, we can continue to relax. We will not need to monitor their daily progress as they learn the various skills of reading, writing, and arithmetic. We will not need to stand over them while they do their homework (or, as is becoming more and more common, doing their homework for them). We will not need to design their science projects. All of that is their responsibility.

So just be the very best parents that you can be. Teach through the real life situations, the every day conversations, the spontaneous parenting moments, the role modeling that occur naturally in the course of your daily activities together. Create a home environment that maximizes the potential for those natural real life situations to turn into positive parenting moments. And teach through them.

Now, none of this is meant to suggest that a wall of separation should be erected between ourselves and our children's schooling. Far from it- as our children's parents, we are called upon to show real interest in their little world, including their schooling. And we will no doubt find it appropriate from time to time to offer assistance with homework and school projects. But when we do so, we will be most effective in our efforts to raise our children for success and happiness in school if we assume the role of the coach, exploring and guiding, rather than that of the teacher, directing and explaining.

Now let's get specific. In trying to be the very best parents that we can be, and in trying to teach our children through naturally occurring experiences, what specifically should we be doing in the home to most effectively raise our children for success and happiness in school? Are there some specific attitudes and values that we should be striving to make our own? Are there some specific behaviors that we should strive to model? And if so, what are they?

What follows are three specific behaviors that I have observed over the years that appear to maximize a child's potential for finding success and happiness in school. Although there is abundant research from various sources to support these behaviors, I know of no research that has identified them as a group, and my selection of them is not based on whatever research does support them. I am sure there are other behaviors that are supported by research, and, on that criterion, might be included here.

Rather, I list these behaviors because I have observed their effectiveness over the years. Over and over again, student after student, family after family, I have seen these behaviors when practiced yield wonderful results; when ignored, unnecessary problems.

The three behaviors- Contribution, Affirmation, and Emotional Stability- build on the Significant Seven perceptions and skills introduced in the previous chapter and address the question of what specifically we parents need to be doing to provide the optimum home environment for our children to experience success and happiness in school. They focus clearly not on what the school can do to ensure the most effective learning environment (another subject entirely), but on what we parents can do.

There is much in American schooling that needs to be changed. There are great teachers and not so great teachers . . . and a few who have no business at all being in the classroom. There are administrators who have the needs of the children and families uppermost in their minds, and there are those whose only concern is getting through the day without a crisis, or satisfying a politically-oriented school board, or retiring in peace. That is reality, and there is probably very little we can do to change it. But we *can* focus on what *we* can do in the home, and we can resolve to be the very best parents that we can be. And I am convinced that if we practice these three behaviors, we will go a long way toward preparing our children for success and happiness in school.

It has been my experience that children raised in a home in which all family members participate in chores come to school more willing and eager to assume their school responsibilities and take an active part in their own education; those who are not tend to expect things to be done for them, and when they are not, struggle to learn the habit of work, a habit they should have learned at home. Children who are raised in a home in which their own interests and talents are affirmed and supported tend to come to school anxious to further develop those interests and talents and tend to be more open to finding new interests and talents; those who are not tend to be resentful of the script their parents wrote for them and either become compliant and passive recipients of learning, which they see as just more of the same script, or rebels who reject school entirely. And children raised in a home characterized by emotional stability and support come to school happy, receptive, and anxious to participate in this new community called a classroom; those who are not come anticipating more stress, more dislocation, and more failed communication, and, predictably, find it.

Will these three behaviors guarantee straight 'A's on the report card? Will they necessarily result in placement on the Honor Roll? Will they ensure acceptance into an Ivy League university? No. But they *will* provide the most supportive home environment possible, an environment in which they will learn the importance of being a responsible member of a community, feel affirmed in their uniqueness, and experience emotional stability in an increasingly unstable world. And that will allow them to start school with the habit of cooperation and the value of contribution firmly entrenched, with an appreciation and respect for individual differences, and with a predisposition for reasoned problem solving through communication. All of which will result in a much more successful, and happy, school experience than if they did not receive the benefit of those behaviors.

So let's learn these three behaviors and make them our own. Let's maximize our children's school experience. Let's give them the best head start we can. Let's be the very best parents we can be.

CHAPTER 4

CONTRIBUTION:
ORGANIZING THE FAMILY FOR HOUSEHOLD CHORES

"Who will help me bake the bread?" said the little Red Hen.
"Not I!" said the duck.
"Not I!" said the goose.
"Not I!" said the cat.
"Not I!" said the pig.

-The Little Red Hen

The first behavior that I have found to increase the potential for success and happiness in school is the creation of a home environment in which chores are a natural and expected part of the child's life. Chores teach responsibility, the importance of completing tasks, the distinction between wants and needs, time management, a sense of belonging and significance in the family, and a host of related "real-life" lessons. If school is meant to be preparation for the real world, then household chores are preparation for schooling, particularly for that part of schooling that includes class work and homework.

For many of us, chores is a dirty word. It conjures up memories of raking leaves, baling hay, washing windows, cleaning garages, and other unpleasantries. But one child's unpleasantry is another child's contribution. It's all a matter of perception.

Many years ago, when I was in college, I had the opportunity to experience how one person can perceive an activity as a chore and another can experience it as an exciting opportunity. A city boy from a metropolis numbering in the millions, I went away to college at age seventeen and was teamed up with a roommate from a small dairy town with a population counted in two digits. When Thanksgiving came and we had a few extra days off, I joined my roommate and his family at their home for my first introduction to farming life. Guess who was the first to wake up each morning at 4:30, filled with excitement and expectation, to milk the cows. For my roommate, it was a drudgery he had been doing, morning after morning and evening after evening, all his life; for me, it was new, exciting, and fun. It's all a matter of perception.

Marian was raised in a family in which her mom included her in as many household activities as possible. Her earliest memories center around the many things that they did together, both work and play, much of it indistinguishable. One of her earliest memories is of her mother and her doing the family wash together. Although only two or three years old at the time and now some thirty years in the past, Marian's picture of the event remains vivid. Mom's job was to take the wet clothes out of the washing machine and hand them to Marian, waiting expectantly next to her. Marian would then place the pile of wet clothes in the dryer, close the door tightly, press the start button, and stand back in pride for a job well done. Growing up, Marian was convinced that it took two to do the family wash. For her, working with her mother was no chore; it was a contribution.

Marian's mom was very wise. She knew intuitively that Marian would perceive herself as a significant, contributing member of the family if she was given opportunities to work *with* her, as an asset. Marian was not treated by her mom as an object of her direction being ordered around the house, or a recipient of her "doing for," as if she were not capable of contributing, but as a real asset in the family, someone without whom the work could simply not be done.

And Mom involved her early on in life, when she was anxious to demonstrate her capability and importance in the family. We often miss those opportunities to involve our children when they are most anxious to be involved, dismissing their efforts because we think they are too young, or because we feel it will take too long to train them, or because it just isn't worth the hassle to bother with them. Thankfully, Marian's mom ignored the temptation to take the easy path and do it all herself, and instead channeled her enthusiasm to be involved and to contribute into a cooperative relationship around the house. Today, Marian, a teacher, continues the lessons she learned growing up by providing collaborative learning opportunities and classroom responsibilities for her students so that they might see themselves as contributing members of their classroom community.

Not all of us are as intuitively wise as Marian's mom. When my
son, Thomas, was seven, he approached me outside while I was
mowing the lawn. To the eyes of a seven-year-old, the whole
business of mowing a lawn is perceived quite differently from those
of thirty-year-old. To Thomas, it all looked quite exciting. The
whirr of the motor, the blades of grass flying out from beneath the
machine, the attraction of participating in "men's work," the very
ritual of the Saturday morning activity all excited him, and he ran
outside, anxious to participate.

"Dad, let me help. Watch me. I can do it." His anticipation was
palpable. His interest in participating was resolute. His desire to
contribute and show me that he was a capable young person were
undisguised. He was young, innocent, and anxious to be my helper.
And I shut him out.

"Thomas, I'm very busy," I replied. "I really don't have time to let you do it now. If you really want to help, go inside and leave me alone."

"But, Dad, I really *do* know how to do it. Come on, just let me do a few rows. I'm not going to hurt the grass. Just let me do a little." Thomas gave it his best shot, so anxious to show me what he could do, so anxious to participate with his dad in the Saturday morning ritual of cutting the lawn, so anxious to show me that he was emerging as a young man himself.

"If you really want to help, Thomas, you'll go inside and play," I replied, stubbornly resisting his efforts to become a larger part of my life. "Or you'll go watch television. But you really need to leave me alone. I'm very busy."

By the time Thomas had reached fourteen, I had grown weary of mowing the lawn. I decided it was time to involve him in the activity. This was "men's work," after all, and, at fourteen, he was becoming a young man, and so I had decided it was time he assumed the lawn maintenance responsibilities.

I approached him with my brainstorm, reminded him that he had many times asked to do the lawn with me, and told him that I had decided that it was time for him to take over. His response was unexpected, but understandable. In his own little inarticulate way, he let me know how he felt: "Dad, seven years ago I went outside and offered to help. I was anxious to be part of what you were doing, but you said no. You told me to go inside and play. You told we to go watch television. Well, I've been working at that for the past seven years now, and I've really gotten good at it. I've really got it down now. Sorry."

Luckily for me, Thomas decided shortly later that he wanted to earn some money through his own efforts, and so he started looking for neighbors who needed their lawns cut. We made a deal: We would give him the initial equipment he would need- mower, edger, extension cords, etc.- and he would take care of our lawn as well as that of his growing list of customers. Twenty-two years old now, Thomas has to date purchased two new cars and helped to finance a college education with the money he has earned cutting other people's lawns.

Thomas is entrepreneurial by nature, and his work ethic has always been strong. Because of these innate factors, he survived my poor example. In another child, in other circumstances, the results could have been disastrous. Even for a child with great potential, shutting him out, failing to involve him in our activities, if done over and over again, might very well result in negative, long-lasting perceptions.

Chores provide an excellent, perhaps essential, training ground for successful schooling, particularly as it relates to school assignments, an important part of which is homework. Since the whole business of involving the family in household chores is more successful when it is planned, organized, and structured than when it is simply assumed, it is very much to our purpose to spend some time examining more effective ways to raise children with chores. Following that, we will address the issue of homework, a source of continuing frustration in families with school-age children.

CHORES

Why Chores?

I have some friends who are quite wealthy. In fact, they are self-made millionaires. They are pioneers in the grocery store business, and they earned their millions building successful chains, selling them, and then building even more successful chains. Involving their children in household chores is the last thing they ever needed to do: maids, cooks, and groundskeepers could have easily been hired, sparing their children from the drudgery of chores. But maids, cooks, and groundskeepers were foreign to their household. Their children participated with them in all their household chores and, when they were old enough, took outside jobs in local restaurants and grocery stores, just like their middle class neighbors. Raising their children to know the importance of being part of the home economy was just too important a value for them. Their children would not be deprived of the life lessons of family chores.

Chores teach children that they are important to the family. Indeed it can be said that depriving children of the opportunity to do chores and instead doing everything for them teaches them that they are not needed in the family, not needed by their parents, that they can only be takers in life, not givers. And the more that we do for them, the more they tend to perceive that they we do not need them. These are far from healthy perceptions to develop.

Chores give children opportunities to perceive themselves as contributing members of the family. Chores communicate to them, much as they did for Marian, that they are needed, that things would just not run as smoothly as they do without them, that the household would be incomplete without their involvement.

Chores teach children the importance of following through on a task to its completion. They teach time management, responsibility, and self-discipline. They help develop the basic work skills that are needed by all of us, at home, at school, on the job, and in the community.

Chores teach that there is a distinction between wants and needs, and that sometimes, for the good of the community (in this case, the family), what we *need* to do must be chosen over what we *want* to do. This lesson, the importance of the good of the community, has implications for the child's appreciation of something Austrian psychologist Alfred Adler called 'social interest.' Adler, the inspiration for today's positive discipline approaches in family and school discipline, emphasized the importance of seeing oneself as part of a greater community to which we owed involvement, participation, and service. Chores help young children internalize a sense of this 'social interest' from their earliest years.

And- lest we forget!- chores for children make maintaining the household that much easier for us parents. But this may well be the least important benefit of chores. Responsibility, self-discipline, time management, task completion, the perception of significance, 'social interest'- even if chores for children added nothing to household cleanliness and neatness they would have value in and of themselves. Maybe the best way to say it is simply this: If you want your child to become responsible, then give him responsibilities.

Organizing the Family for Household Chores

OK, so chores are good for kids. So just how can we organize
our family for them, without constant hassles?

First of all, it's important to understand that what we want to do is
organize the *whole* family for work. That includes Mom, each of
the children, and, yes, Dad. Several years ago, we had an
emergency family meeting on chores. Carol, a kindergarten teacher
and therefore the hardest working individual on earth, felt that she
was being expected to take on too much of the responsibility for the
household chores. And she was right. So we sat down as a family,
wrote out all the chores, discussed the several options available,
came to an agreement through consensus, and went to work. (I
ended up with responsibility for cooking dinners; you should know
that ever since we have developed a fondness for take-out pizza.)

There are a number of ways to successfully organize the family for

99

chores. Tom Sawyer had his own way. He conned a friend into painting the fence by feigning enthusiasm for the job. The good news is that that trick does work . . . in the short run. After all, the fence did get painted. But Tom would never be able to pull off that same con with that same friend again. So what we need to look for are long-term ways to involve the family in household chores, ways that if not effective in involving all members enthusiastically will at least involve all members out of a sense of responsibility to the family community. Some ways that have been found effective by many families include the following:

• Provide choices

We adults appreciate it when we are allowed choices in life about what we want to do, how we want to do it, and when we want to do it. Children also should be provided that same courtesy. Please note that choices come within limits. In the family community, there are no choices about whether or not each family member is going to participate in the household chores. That is a given. But how each member participates is up for discussion. A very respectful and effective way to do this might be as follows: "Jackie, since we have guests coming over tomorrow you will need to clean your room. Would you like to clean it tonight or early tomorrow morning?" Notice that there is no debate about Jackie's need to participate in household chores (and no debate about who is responsible for this particular chore, since it is her room), but she is given a choice regarding when to do it.

• Make games of the selection process

Many families find that making games of the process of selecting chores is an effective way to involve children. A variant of the old truth that "a spoonful of sugar helps the medicine go down," this is probably most effective with very young children. Some families I have worked with in parenting situations have told me about spinning wheels they have created with the family chores identified in each segment. Each week each family member spins the spinner to find out what his chores for that week will be. The chores would be simple ones that each family member could do, such as sweeping the back patio, cleaning off the table after dinner, dusting the furniture, etc. Adding this little bit of fun and anticipation into the selection process appears to make it all that much more acceptable.

• Do the chores together as a family

Whenever possible, do the chores together as a family. Raking the backyard leaves is far more enjoyable if it is done as a family project involving all family members. Establishing a weekly chore time during which all the chores are done by all family members can also help eliminate the drudgery and sense of aloneness that makes chores less than enjoyable.

• Schedule the chores

Whether or not you are able to do the chores together as a family, be sure to schedule them. We all work best with schedules- at home as well as on the job. Provide your children with planning schedules to post in their rooms, or, better yet, encourage them to devise planning schedules on their own. Let them be creative in decorating and designing their own planning schedule. And have a master schedule posted somewhere in the common family area. A posted schedule with reminders of which days are garbage days and which days are sweep-the-patio days is far more effective than continual nagging. And it teaches the importance of scheduling and planning your activities and responsibilities, a skill that many adults still struggle with.

• Create a family chore chart

Many families have found that a posted family chore chart serves well as a reminder about chores, reducing the nagging that only adds frustration to the whole business of chores. This could vary from a simple listing of family names on a poster or chalk board with the chores of the week written below to a more creative and elaborate system involving peg boards or magnetic displays. Involving the children in creating the display would further encourage their participation in the chores.

• Don't "fix" the job the child has done

Avoid as much as possible the temptation to "fix" the job the child has done. Yes, we can probably clean the room better than the child can, and if a clean room is our only goal than we might as well just go ahead and clean it ourselves. But if our goal is the raising of a child who will learn responsibility, contribution, cooperation, and the basic skills of straightening a messy room, than we need to get him involved in the process.

So let's avoid following our children around "fixing" their mistakes. Straightening out the bed covers on the bed he has made, or picking up leaves in the backyard that he has missed, only communicates to the child that he is not really an asset to the family and that he is not as capable as we would like. It sends the message that I will let you participate in the chores of the house, but, frankly, you're not really capable of doing the kind of job I expect so I'll be right behind you fixing it. And using positive words- "Oh, how nice the bed looks!"- while "fixing" the job doesn't help; our children may hear the words, but our actions speak so much louder. It may take some effort on our part, but we can learn to live with a less-than-perfectly-made bed. We can say to ourselves, OK, the bed isn't made up just the way I would like it to be, but I can take pride that my little five-year-old made up that bed to the best of her ability all by herself, and I applaud her efforts.

• Recognize that it takes time for training

One reason we often prefer to do it all ourselves, rather than involving our children, is because it takes time to train them. But what we fail to recognize is that the time it takes to train them now will pay off in the long run- in the long run, we will have less to do ourselves, and, more importantly, our children will have been raised in a home in which they have learned that responsibilities are an expected part of life. Taking time for training simply means breaking the chore down into manageable parts, explaining what needs to be accomplished in each part, giving some tips on how best to accomplish it (but allowing for individual differences and choices), and giving specific feedback about the result. Doing one's wash, something a child can learn to do very early on, can be broken down into separating whites from colors, placing the clothes into the washer, selecting the proper temperature and time setting, pouring in the detergent, closing the lid, and pressing the start button. Each of these steps will take time and practice, and our patience with occasional mistakes, but that time and practice will pay off in the long run.

• Show appreciation by using "I" messages

There is much debate going on today about the negative effects of statements of praise (as opposed to statements of encouragement, appreciation, or affirmation), and to what extent these are more semantic squabbles than real differences of opinion is very much a part of that debate. But there should be little doubt that there are expressions that we can use to show our appreciation that effectively do that, and there are expressions that we can use that communicate very different messages. I can tell my daughter that she is a good girl for cleaning her room, or I can tell her that I am pleased with the way she cleaned her room because now I can leave her door open when our guests arrive. The first may suggest to her that her worthiness depends upon what she does and how well she does it- if she did not clean her room, would that make her a bad girl? The second simply communicates to her my feelings about the job that she has done, with no inference that the quality of the job defines her goodness or badness.

The second expression used above is an example of what are called "I" messages, statements that communicate clearly, specifically, and honestly how *I* feel about what was done. In using "I" messages, I accept ownership of my feeling, I communicate it honestly, I explain why I feel that way, and, if necessary, I give clear indication of what still needs to be done. If my daughter failed to clean her room, I could say: "Jennifer, I am very displeased (my feeling) that you did not clean your room as you had agreed to (honest communication) because our friends were looking forward to seeing our home (explanation of why I am displeased); therefore, you will need to stop watching television right now and attend to your room (clear indication of what needs to be done). No implication that Jennifer's personhood is being evaluated, no use of adultisms, no blaming or criticizing, just a clear statement pointing out what was not done and how the matter must now be addressed. Try using "I" messages the next time you want to communicate your feelings- you will feel better about it and so will your children.

• Use family meetings to provide opportunities for discussion about chores and responsibilities

How to establish and run family meetings will be addressed more fully in Chapter 6, "Emotional Stability: Providing a Safe Haven in the Home"; for now, suffice it to say that when all members of a family sit down together on a regular basis to discuss family needs with a spirit of openness, and resolve issues through consensus building rather than through executive edict, then children are more willing to participate.

Allowances and Chores

The question of whether or not to give children allowances for chores always reminds me of the Iran-Contra hearings back in the late '80s. Remember Lt. Colonel Oliver North and the Senate investigating committee inquiring into allegations that the United States government had sold arms to Iran in exchange for the release of our hostages, and then diverted the money to the Contras in Nicaragua? It was all very complicated, but those being accused of wrongdoing kept insisting that the deal to sell the arms to their Iranian contacts had nothing to do with the deal to get them to release our hostages. Did you sell arms to the Iranian militants? Yes. Did they then release our hostages? Yes. So you sold them arms so that they would release the hostages. Well, no, not exactly.

What does that have to do with allowances for chores? Frankly, it's a weasel way of introducing a topic of much debate among those in the business of advising parents on raising their children. Neale S. Godfrey and Carolina Edwards, in *Money Doesn't Grow on Trees,* argue that allowances should definitely be given for chores. In the real world, our work is compensated with financial reward, so why not do so for children? They will learn the value of a dollar, the worthiness of work, and the relationship between effort put in and results obtained.

On the other hand, Alfie Kohn, author of *Punished by Rewards: The Trouble with Gold Stars, Incentive Plans, A's, Praise, and Other Bribes,* cites numerous examples of how pay actually *reduces* the quality of work, since it suggests that the work has no value in and of itself but only in terms of the pay attached to it. Since the work has no intrinsic value, why do anything more than just what is needed to get the promised pay? Kohn further argues against communicating to children that chores, which should be done as part of one's responsibility as a member of the family community, should be recognized with a financial reward.

My own feeling on this is much closer to Kohn's: If we really want to raise our children to see themselves as contributing members of the family, and later as contributing members of their classroom, work place, and civic communities, then we should divorce the issue of allowances from the issue of household responsibilities. By all means, let's give our children allowances, but let's not communicate that the allowances are rewards for doing what they should be doing as contributing members of the family community.

Why then give them allowances, if not for the chores that they do? Because as members of the family community, children should share in the resources of that community. Because one of the most important lessons in life to learn is how to manage resources. Because allowing children to make financial decisions early in life in safe, supportive settings- and allowing them to experience the consequences of those decisions- will give them practice and training as they grow up and face tougher and more lasting financial decisions. Because if they have their own money, they can practice the habits of spending wisely, saving for future needs, and even giving some to charitable causes as part of their responsibility to be of service.

Should we never compensate our children for work done around the house? For their normal daily and weekly chores, I would argue no- these should be done as part of their responsibilities to the family. But there are often jobs around the house that we sometimes pay others to do, and a good rule of thumb in considering pay for work around the house might be this: If you would otherwise pay someone outside the home to do a certain job, then pay your children for doing it. This might include lawn maintenance, "deluxe" style car cleaning, long-term baby-sitting, and painting, to name just a few of our less-than-exciting home responsibilities. If your normal course of action would be to hire someone else to do a job, consider offering it to your children for pay. That way they will learn both of the lessons espoused by Godfrey and Edwards, on the one hand, and Kohn, on the other: They will learn that there are jobs around the house that we do because we are members of the family community, and then there are other jobs that go beyond those normal household responsibilities, jobs that we prefer to pay others to do, and so now we have the opportunity to do them, earn extra income, and learn the "real world" value of work for pay. Valuable lessons on both counts.

How early should we start giving our children allowances? As soon as they start asking us to buy them things. The first time a child asks a parent to buy him something is an excellent teachable moment to talk about allowances. It's a perfect time to tell our child that toys are given for special occasions, like birthdays, but otherwise, if you want something, you will have to save your allowance and buy it yourself. We will provide you with an allowance because you are a member of the family and should share in the family resources, and we will provide guidance about spending and saving, and now you will have the opportunity to make choices about the things you want.

In short, there are plenty of excellent reasons to give our children allowances without the need to tie those allowances directly to chores. Let's give them allowances, and let's involve them in household chores, but let's strive to keep those two as separate as possible.

Real Chores

Often we shortchange our children by assuming that they can't do something they are perfectly capable of doing. In my experience working with parents, I have learned numerous ways that we can involve our children in real life chores and activities, and in doing so communicate to them that they are capable and significant young people who are true assets in the family . . . and who don't just get stuck with the grunge chores that Mom and Dad don't want to do. The story of Marian and the washing machine wonderfully demonstrates this, and it should serve as encouragement for us in our efforts to introduce our children early to the world of chores and contributions. My own failure to involve my son at age seven in cutting the grass was presented as another example, this time of what not to do. A number of other examples of involving our children in real chores, chores that communicate to them that they are real contributors to the family, follows:

• In one family, the twelve-year-old son is responsible for clipping grocery coupons from the newspapers and organizing them for use while shopping. In addition to performing a valuable service for his parents, he is learning about comparative shopping, various pricing methods, quantity buying, weighing quantity vs. quality, and the value of saving money. And he enjoys the opportunity to be with his mom or dad when they do the shopping, pointing out the better bargains and taking pride in the money he is saving the family.

• In another family, the parents have taught their four-year-old to scramble eggs. Every meal time at their home is a cooperative experience, with Dad, Mom, and each child contributing to the preparation of the meal, the setting of the table, and the clean-up. Their four-year-old has taken a real liking to scrambled eggs for breakfast instead of cold cereal ever since he was allowed to scramble them himself.

• A third family used the issue of whether or not to get a family pet, in this case a dog, to involve their six-year-old in real life chores. Jessie would get a dog if she would promise to feed him and take him for walks, and she could keep the dog only so long as she continued to do so. She made the promise, she followed through, and she learned real life lessons about responsibility, caring for another, and self-discipline in the process.

• And in a fourth family, the fourteen-year-old daughter keeps the family checkbook, making the deposits and paying the bills. In doing so, she is learning all about utility bills, mortgage payments, the cost of food, etc., as well as the larger issues of budgeting, saving, deferred gratification, and financial responsibilities.

Chores and Morning Hassles

Of all the minor irritants that trouble parents today, morning hassles has got to top the list, at least if discussion at my parenting classes is an accurate indicator. Getting the children up and dressed, struggling with breakfast, brushing teeth, finding backpacks and tennis shoes and reports that are due first thing in the morning . . . all this can lead to a stressful morning and a poor start for the kids in school and for Mom and Dad at work. Getting off to a peaceful, hassle-free, well organized start in the morning does matter, so let's take a look at the morning hassles that often result in our children starting their school day at less than their best, and see if we can identify ways to change the negative morning experience into a positive one.

Viewed from the perspective of household chores, the morning responsibilities that result in morning hassles are no more difficult to get a handle on than any other responsibilities. We just need to treat them as we would treat all household responsibilities, so let's look back at what we have learned and see what ideas would apply specifically to morning hassles:

- Use family meetings to discuss and clarify all responsibilities and concerns about morning hassles; make sure all family members are allowed to give their input into the problem; brainstorm and make a list of all ideas that can help the morning go more smoothly.

- Help your children design posters or charts for their room that will serve as reminders about their morning responsibilities; the more interaction they have with the chart, the better- a chart that necessitates their checking items off on a daily basis is more effective than one that just lists the items they need to do.

- Take time for training by helping your children learn organizational skills, suggesting how they might lay out their clothes for the next day and where to place their book bag and other materials, for example; make sure each child has his own alarm clock and knows how to use it.

- Provide choices for morning responsibilities that involve the whole family; setting the table for breakfast, for example, provides opportunities for choices among the various activities- placing the dishes and silverware, getting the cereal, milk, and juice, cleaning the table when everyone is finished, etc.; use family meetings to provide a format for the choices.

• Set aside time at the end of each day to talk about the next day and what will be needed to be ready for it.

• Make it a point for all family members to have responsibilities in the morning, just as at other times, to reemphasize that chores are a total family affair.

• Avoid distractions like TV and video games that not only provide temptations to ignore morning responsibilities but also disrupt what few moments are available in the morning for family bonding.

As parents, it is our responsibility to provide the atmosphere and routine that will minimize morning hassles. But the more we can involve our children in that task, the better. It's not easy, but the benefit to both our children and us of a smooth morning, which carries over to a smoother day and evening, is well worth the effort.

The benefits to the home of involving and organizing children for chores are a closer, more mutually respectful, more involved, and more committed family whose members see themselves as critical to the success of the family community. The benefits to the child include those attitudes and skills- time management, responsibility, task completion, etc.- that are valued so much in the world of work. But before the world of work there is the world of schooling . . . and homework. And nothing can better prepare a student for the world of class assignments and homework than family chores.

Homework can be a source of agony in families. It can also be a source of achievement, as we see our children take responsibility for what is required of them. Unfortunately today, many parents deprive their children of the opportunity to learn the many previously-mentioned skills by doing everything for them, and then follow the same pattern with homework. Teachers throughout our country routinely complain about parents who do their children's homework for them. It is an issue very much worth our attention.

HOMEWORK

Let's tell it straight, right up front: Homework is between the teacher and the student. It is not between the teacher and the parent.

Homework is the student's job. It is his opportunity to learn self-discipline, defined here as the habit of doing what one needs to do rather than what one wants to do. It is his opportunity to learn responsibility, time management, and the empowering sense of achievement that attends to the conclusion of difficult tasks. It is the child's first opportunity to experience accountability to someone other than his parents. To rob our children of these opportunities would be a serious mistake. And yet, in the name of love, we so often do so.

A teacher once received the following note from a mom about her seventh grade child:

"We did not have time to study for the history test last night. We looked up the answers and did the vocabulary. Can we take the test tomorrow?"

We did not have time to study for the history test? *We* looked up the answers and did the vocabulary? Can *we* take the test tomorrow? Who is the student here?

Or as reported in the January 1996 <u>Readers' Digest:</u>

"As an English teacher at Marana High School in Tucson, Arizona, I thought I had heard every story about late or missing homework. Then one afternoon a parent walked into my class, handed some papers to her daughter, and said, 'I just finished it. I hope it's not too late for you to turn in.' "

One is tempted to ask if that parent shows up on test day to take her daughter's exams as well.

Or how about this classic, from Ann Landers' April 4, 1996, column:

"I have worked in the same company for over 12 years and have always had a comfortable working relationship with my boss and my colleagues. Yesterday, my boss brought his daughter's fourth grade homework assignment to me and asked that I or one of my assistants type it up. After much consideration, I walked into his office and told him I thought it was inappropriate for him to ask this. I explained that he was doing a grave disservice to his daughter by not insisting she complete her own homework. I told him I would not do his child's homework, but since he was the boss, I would ask someone else to do it if he so demanded . . . Today, I found out he personally asked my assistant to complete his daughter's homework . . ."

Hmmm . . . just who is the real boss here?

Resisting the temptation to get too involved in our child's homework is, indeed, difficult. When they come to us with homework questions- "What were the causes of the Civil War?", "How do you pronounce this word?"- we are strongly tempted to give the quick answer that will satisfy their immediate need and allow us to get back to our newspaper, TV show, or house work with minimal distraction. But that only serves to communicate two negative messages: one, we don't have time to give serious attention to our children and, two, they are incapable of taking the necessary steps to solve their own problems. So let's consider some alternative approaches.

One approach would be to tell our children that their homework is none of our concern, that it's their responsibility, that we paid our homework dues years ago, that we're deeply involved in the newspaper, and please don't bother us again. While this may indeed communicate that homework is the child's responsibility, this approach, a good example of hostile permissiveness, communicates also that we are unconcerned about our child's needs. Is the child empowered to do his best in this scenario?

An alternative approach, one that avoids hostile permissiveness and communicates, instead, genuine concern, while at the same time empowering the child to have faith in her own abilities, might be demonstrated by the following conversation:

Marcia: "Dad, how do you pronounce this word?"
Dad: "Well, honey, let me take a look here. That's a tough one. I can see why you would have difficulty with it. What tricks have you learned in school to help you sound out a word?
Marcia: "We're supposed to break it down part by part and sound out each part and then put them back together, but it isn't working for this one."
Dad: "Well, why don't you give it a try. I'll listen carefully and help you if you get stuck. Go ahead."

Let's take a look at this. What perceptions might the child develop from this exchange? That she is a significant enough person that her dad will give her his attention? That she is a capable enough person who with a little coaching and guidance can solve her own problems? That this family environment is a safe one for asking questions, making mistakes, and learning? One would have to argue in the affirmative on all three.

Note also that Dad is not communicating to Marcia that sounding out the word is easy. By communicating to her that he can understand why she would be having difficulty, he is showing respect for her struggle and validating her efforts. In doing so, he is creating a safe place for Marcia to share her concerns, which today may only be about homework but tomorrow may be about boy friend problems or drugs in school or career choices. Dad is communicating to Marcia, very early on, that he is available for her to share whatever concerns she has. He will not solve her problems for her, but he will listen empathically, offer guidance, and affirm her in her struggles.

Or consider this conversation:

Robbie: "Mom, what were the causes of the Civil War?"

Mom: "Well, that sounds like a good homework question. Where do you think you might find the answer?"

Robbie: (not in the mood for Mom's parenting class response) "I don't know. I left my social studies book in school. Just tell me the answer."

Mom: (unruffled) "Well, what other books or resources do we have around the house that might be helpful here?"

Robbie: (clearly annoyed now) "I don't know. Just give me the answer. It will save time for both of us."

Mom: (not taking the bait) "Yes, it would save time for both of us . . . in the short run. But I care for you too much to deprive you of the opportunity to use your own abilities to solve this problem, so let me try again. Where else might you be able to find the answer to your question than in your social studies book?"

Robbie: (really irritated now) "Things were so much easier around here before you started going to those stupid parenting classes! Forget it. I'll just go ask Dad. Dad, what were the causes of the Civil War?"

Dad: (wisely taking the cue from Mom) "Well, that sounds like a good homework question. Where do you think you might find the answer?"

Robbie: (angrily stomping off in the direction of the bookshelf holding the encyclopedias) "Forget it. I'll just look it up in the encyclopedia."

Mom and Dad: (together, in more ways than one) "Great idea. Let us know how it works out."

What is Mom (and Dad, who also took the parenting course) doing here? She is refusing to rescue her child and, instead, is continuing to put the ball back in his court. She is respectfully validating his efforts, but she is also declining to take responsibility away from him. She is communicating confidence in his ability to solve his own problems. And she does not allow Robbie's anger to become a separate, distracting issue.

The first step in solving homework hassles is the recognition that homework is the student's responsibility, not the parents'. If we consistently follow through on that, supporting our children's efforts and offering guidance where appropriate in the process, we

118

have effectively laid the foundation for a more pleasant experience with homework. But there is much more to this issue of homework than just recognizing that it is the child's responsibility, not the parents', so let's take a look now at several specific areas of concern that continue to surface regarding this important aspect of schooling.

School-Smart Parenting Tip

Homework is the child's responsibility, not the parents'.
If we start enforcing that early, with encouragement,
empathy, and support, we will lay the foundation for our
children's development as capable young people who
understand the meaning of personal responsibility.

"Homework is so boring!"

I once had a history professor who would say that to the interesting person, everything is interesting; to the boring person, everything is boring. My children have never reacted favorably to my quoting that, so it's probably not a very effective approach.

Yes, it would be wonderful if homework could always be exciting. It would be wonderful if all chores could be exciting, and all jobs in the "real world" could be exciting, and all our varied responsibilities as parents, spouses, employees and employers could be exciting. But that will never be the case. So it's probably more effective to just accept the fact that, yes, homework may very well be boring at times, and move on from there, confident that there are some very good reasons for homework, boring though it may be.

Why homework? In the early school years, homework is given

largely to provide opportunities for children to learn responsibility and study habits. Reinforcement of skills is very much secondary to the more important goal of developing the habits that will serve the child so well in later years.

In the middle grades, reinforcement of knowledge and skills becomes the primary value of homework, with the continuing development of responsibility and study habits a close second. Not until the later years, college and graduate school, does personal enrichment and discovery become the primary values for homework. But without the development of the habits of responsibility and studying in the early years, that opportunity for personal and enrichment may never occur.

When to Do Homework

Let's face it: We adults are not all alike when it comes to energy level. Why should we expect our children to be? Some of us are morning people; others don't get started until 10:00 or 11:00.

I'm a morning person. Typically, I'm up at 4:45, out the door for a morning jog by 5:45, and at work by 7:30. I have a friend who swears he's never seen 4:45 A.M. and even doubts that there is such a thing. He struggles out of bed at 8:00, is at work by 9:00, . . . and wakes up some time around 10:30. By 3:00, when I'm placing tooth picks in my eyes to keep them open, he's enjoying his daily exercise routine. By 10:00, he's ready to hit the town. And I'm setting my alarm for the next morning.

We all have different internal clocks, and we need to respect them in our children, just as we respect them in adults. When is the best time to do homework? For some, it will be right after school. For others, just before or just after dinner. Some will prefer late at night just before retiring. And for still others, in the morning before going to school. We parents need to respect that and allow for differences. How can we demonstrate that respect? The following dialogue, which might take place very effectively in a beginning-of-the-year family meeting, might help:

Dad: "Here's an interesting agenda item- homework. Rebecca, what are your plans for doing your homework this year?"

Rebecca: "Well, last year I did it right after school because I found that I got too distracted with telephone calls later in the evening, but I don't think that will work this year because of track practice. I think I'll try to get on a right-after-dinner schedule."

Dad: "What problems might that cause you with telephone calls and other distractions?"

Rebecca: "I'm going to tell my friends not to call me until after 8:00 . . . and use my message recorder for those who forget!"

Dad: "Sounds like a great idea. Let me know how it works."

What if our children demonstrate difficulty making an effective choice? How can we help guide them while at the same time respecting their need to make choices? Let's look at the following dialogue:

Dad: "Andy, what are your plans for doing your homework this year?"

Andy: "Oh, I'll probably do it just before going to bed. That's when I did it last year."

Dad: "Well, how did that work out last year? I seem to recall some communication from the school regarding missed homework."

Andy: "Yeah, but that was just during soccer season when we had those late night games . . . And during basketball season when the coach had those late meetings . . . And during . . . Well, maybe right after school would be a better idea."

Dad: "How do you feel right after school? Do you need a break of any kind?"

Andy: "I like to get a quick snack. After that I think I can get right to my homework."

Dad: "Great idea. And I'd like to pass on something that I heard just the other day about this stuff. If you break up your homework and your studying into smaller chunks, taking occasional breaks here and there, it will turn out better. Apparently, we're more alert at the beginning and the end of our work, so if we can create more beginnings and ends by breaking up the work into several pieces, we retain what we are learning better. You might want to give that a try. Let me know how it all works out."

Notice that Dad was able to exercise his own guidance based on past experience, and a helpful bit of information he recently picked up, but in a respectful manner that continued to allow for individual choices on the part of his son. Notice too that he recognized the plan as his son's and demonstrated an interest in how it would turn out. Offered with sincerity, these and similar comments communicate that the child deserves to be treated with dignity as he works through life's little challenges, a powerful lesson to communicate.

Where to Do Homework

The same principle that addresses the question of when to do homework should govern the question of where and under what circumstances to do homework. How many of us have spent small fortunes on fancy desks and chairs for our children, only to discover that they prefer to read in bed? Some children prefer to work in their rooms; others feel too isolated there, and are much more effective learners at the kitchen table. Some people work best in an environment of total quiet. Others find quiet unnerving and need some background music. In fact, there are some studies that indicate that classical music is particularly helpful in studying, and there is even some evidence that children labeled attention deficit and hyperactive can actually focus better with rock music playing in the background. (Now that I think about it, John, Paul, George, and Ringo were quite instrumental, pardon the pun, in helping me get through much of my high school math homework.)

The bottom line is this: What matters is that the homework is done, according to the style of the child. Learning styles vary immensely, and it is good to remember that what one person sees as distraction another person sees as providing familiarity and comfort.

"What if my child refuses to do his homework?"

Frankly, that's not an option. When to do the homework, how to do the homework, and where to do the homework- those are options. But whether or not the homework is done is not an option.

If we have raised our children with household chores, if we have affirmed them as capable young people, if we have empathically supported their efforts and struggles, if we have communicated interest in their homework without getting overly involved in it, all within an environment characterized by emotional stability, then the odds are remote that they will seriously ignore their homework or any other responsibilities. But if they do experience difficulty fulfilling their homework responsibilities, then go through a mental checklist to try to determine a possible cause. If they have not had experience with household chores, then it's time for a family meeting to discuss the issue. If we have made too big an issue of grades, perhaps even communicating to them that our love for them is somehow tied into the grades they receive, then we need to let go of that and communicate our love unconditionally. If we have shown no interest in their schooling or their homework, they may perceive that it is not important and it's time for us to make the effort to get into their quality world and find out what's going on in their lives. And if we have become too involved, perhaps even doing our children's homework for them, then we need to back off, wean them from their need to depend on us (or wean ourselves from our need to *have* them depend on us), and reaffirm them as capable people who can accomplish things on their own.

In working with our children on this, it is important not to panic and regress to either an overly strict or overly permissive approach. The overly strict approach looks for quick fixes resulting from the authoritarian now-you're-going-to-do-it-my-way attitude. The permissive approach basically says, "I give up. It's not worth the hassle. Do whatever you want. It's your life." The first results at best in short-term improvements with no internal change in the child. The second communicates the message that we no longer care. Neither are effective. Or respectful.

Instead, continue to work on the root causes of the problem, identified above, and be willing to accept the fact that things might even get a bit worse before they get better. Be patient, give choices regarding the incidentals, be firm in communicating the non-negotiables, and be respectful at all times.

But what if my child won't do his homework by himself, continually asking me how to do this and how to do that? Again, look for root causes. Could it be that your child just wants your continuous attention? If so, firmly and respectfully tell him that it is important that he do his work by himself, but as soon as he is finished the two of you will read a story together, or play a game together, or go for a walk, or whatever your favorite activity together is. This communicates that you do want to spend time with him, that you are willing to give him attention when it is appropriate, but that he also has responsibilities that must be done on his own.

There are no short cuts to this. Yes, you can punish your children and ground them and take away all their diversions, but that will only have short-term effects. Those external measures will not develop the self-reliance and responsibility that is needed. For self-reliance and responsibility, we need to provide the long-term approach of effective parenting, not defective punishing. It takes time and commitment . . . and the decision on our part to make changes in our *own* lives so that our children will be inspired to make changes in theirs. We cannot change others; we can only change ourselves.

Homework, Grades, and Rewards

All that we said previously about rewards for chores (allowances) applies equally well to rewards for completed homework or good grades. In short, avoid it at all costs.

Giving rewards for homework or grades communicates to the child that the homework or test or project has no value in and of itself, thereby contributing to the perception that schooling is irrelevant to the real world, except that part of the real world that has to do with rewards for work. One of the major philosophical questions in education deals with the very purpose of schooling. Is its purpose best explained in terms of the classical values of seeking truth, goodness, and beauty? Is its purpose more cultural- for example, promoting the values of the American people? Is it more ethical- to promote what is right and proscribe what is wrong? Is it more utilitarian- teaching the skills necessary to get a job? Is it parental survival- giving us some time each day away from the kids?

No doubt, American education is all of those things. But raising our children with the expectation that they will be rewarded for fulfilling their responsibilities at school narrows the focus considerably by modeling only those aspects of schooling that promote assimilation into the world of work and compensation. If we want our children to experience more from their schooling than the perception that its sole value is to ready them for the world of work, then we would do well to avoid the temptation to reward them for completing their assignments and for getting good grades.

Does this mean that we must avoid all forms of recognition and celebration for our children's school achievements? Not at all. It only means that we should avoid communicating to them that rewards are the expected outcome for all their accomplishments.

Many families that I have worked with over the years have taken that concept to heart and have switched from taking their children out to dinner as a reward for a good report card to taking them out to dinner to celebrate the successful close of the semester, regardless of the grades received. The celebration is the same- in both cases the family goes out to eat. But previously the children perceived that their parents' attention had to be earned by good grades. Now they see the dinner as a family event in celebration of all their efforts, regardless of specific achievement. Earned attention or family celebration- such a small change can make such a huge difference.

The Do's and Don't's of Parental Involvement in Homework

Finally, let's sum up our discussion of homework by reviewing some do's and don't's about parental involvement:

Do's	Don't's
Do show interest in your child's homework by listening to her when she talks about it or asks for help.	Don't get overly involved by doing the homework for the child.
Do communicate empathy for her struggles.	Don't communicate that the homework is easy and she should have learned it three grades ago.
Do communicate that even though the work may be difficult, you still have confidence that she can do it.	Don't communicate that the work is too hard for her, and the teacher should know that she's just a little girl and shouldn't be expected to do such hard work.
Do allow her choices in when, where, and under what conditions she will do her homework.	Don't demand that the homework be done at this specific time, in this specific place, under these specific conditions.
Do offer guidance if she gets stuck, such as, for example, sharing tricks you have learned for completing	Don't communicate that you don't have time to listen to her problems or concerns; after

homework quicker, or resources you have found that might provide the answers she needs.

all, you have problems of your own!

Do recognize her efforts with sincere and specific words of encouragement: "I really like what you did on that science project because you worked on it all by yourself, you learned a lot about nutrition as a result, and you got to teach me some things I didn't know as well."

Avoid meaningless words of praise: "Great science project!" (Why is it great? What did the child learn from it?) Also, avoid rewards for homework or grades as these communicate that the work has little value in itself.

Do take the opportunity of homework to provide that safe place for your child to seek you out and receive comfort and support.

Don't miss the opportunity to have one-on-one time with your child just because you are too busy with TV, the newspaper, or housework.

Will all this necessarily result in a long and lasting love affair between your child and her homework? Of course not. But it will provide a more supportive and encouraging setting for her to test out her own abilities, make her own choices, follow through on her own plans, and take responsibility for a very important part of her schooling. And the lessons she learns from this will carry over into the "real world" of jobs, families, and communities. So let's take ownership of this first behavior in raising children for success and happiness in school, and start today by organizing our family for household chores.

CHAPTER 5

AFFIRMATION:
SHOWING REAL INTEREST IN THE
CHILD'S WORLD

"I didn't turn out to be the baseball player my father wanted
me to be."

-first response to a radio talk show host's question,
"What would be the first line of your autobiography?"

The second behavior that I have found to increase the potential for success and happiness in school is showing real interest in the child's world: his play, his work, his hobbies, his talents, and his school experiences. When we show real interest in the child's own interests we communicate to him that he is a significant person, with unique opportunities to contribute to the family, to the school, and to the larger community. We communicate that he has the right to individuate himself from us, and even though we might have much to share with him from our wisdom and experiences, he too has much to share with us out of his uniqueness. In short, we affirm him as a person in his own right.

I am choosing my words carefully here. In choosing the word 'interest' I am highlighting the importance of getting into the child's world, including his schooling; I am not choosing the word 'involvement,' which has a very different orientation. Interest includes involvement, but involvement does not necessarily include real interest.

Involvement is currently a hot topic in parent/school communication. Educational leaders uniformly stress the importance of getting involved in our children's schools, and most of the literature on parenting appears to recommend the same. We are frequently being urged to attend school functions, join the PTA, show up for parent conferences, get to know the teachers. And teachers routinely list lack of parental involvement among their greatest concerns. All of this is, of course, very much on target.

But I suspect that the emphasis is being placed on the wrong word. Is it really more involvement we want? Is it really that important that we parents be around the school on a regular basis, that we attend every athletics or music practice, that we sit with our child while he completes his homework? Or is it more important that we communicate to our children sincere interest in what they are doing?

No, these two words are not mutually exclusive. We can be both involved and interested. But my fear is that in emphasizing involvement, we might be tempted to forget the real reason why we should get involved in the first place, namely our interest in (as opposed to our 'control over') our children. Let's take a closer look at this.

Interest and Involvement

How important, first, is involvement? In August 1995, the

Family Involvement Partnership for Learning, a coalition of some 140 educational organizations throughout the country, published a challenge to American families and communities to get involved in their schools. In an introduction to their publication, they wrote: "When families, educators, and communities work together, schools get better and children get the quality education they need to lead happy, productive lives." The coalition went on to argue that the more we get involved in our children's schools, the more we will learn what's going on in them, the more we will discover ways to contribute our time and talent to them, and the more we will be able to stay attuned to potential concerns.

No argument there. "Schools are the responsibility of all of us." "There is no commitment without involvement." "It takes a whole village to raise a child." Familiar cliches. But the reason they are cliches is because they are true. No argument.

But is it possible for parents to become over-involved? Is it possible for parents to be so fearful of letting go, so desirous of advancing their own agenda for their children's lives, that they cannot stay away from the school? Educators frequently tell parents that they need to check their children's homework, yet anecdotal evidence abounds that many parents are getting so involved in their children's homework that a good question could be raised as to whether or not it really is the child's work. And our children are being shortchanged in the capability department because of it.

In fact, a good argument could be made that many parents today have become overly involved in almost every aspect of their children's lives. We are too involved in their school activities, too involved in their social activities, too involved in their play. The very concept of "free play" has become all but lost.

We feel guilty if we are not entertaining our children at every moment, or shuttling them around from friend's house to park to movies to mall. We organize their sports activities, their parties, and their games, thereby depriving them of the opportunity to learn organizational skills for themselves. We sign them up for this activity and that activity, filling every moment of their lives with things to do, things largely of our own choosing. And then we wonder why, during those few times that we have neglected to plan their every activity, they tell us that they are bored. Having never had the opportunity to organize their own activities, they have become dependent upon us to provide them for them, and when they are not provided, they are lost . . . and bored.

So I prefer to use the word interest rather than involvement. Rather than recommend that we parents get actively involved in our schools, I recommend that we shift the focus to one of real interest in what our children are learning and doing. Please note that interest does not preclude or supplant involvement. It simply shifts the focus.

The positive results will stay the same. We will learn more about what's going on in the schools, how we can contribute to their success, and what's happening politically that might affect them. But more than that, we will learn about our children. By focusing on sincere interest in our children's lives, we will learn about their unique strengths and talents, their hobbies, their perceptions, their needs, and the special ways they can contribute to the family and school. And we will avoid the temptation of getting too involved and controlling in their lives.

"I didn't turn out to be the baseball player my father wanted me to be."

I was listening to a radio talk show some time ago, and the subject of the program was how to write an autobiography. The host of the show put this question to the listening audience in order to generate call-in responses: What would be the first line of your autobiography? The very first caller responded: "I didn't turn out to be the baseball player my father wanted me to be."

What an incredibly powerful indictment! The first line of this person's autobiography, the statement that for him sums up his entire life, is that he didn't fulfill the agenda that his father had prescribed for him. His entire life is summarized in terms of a great disappointment, a disappointment resulting from his father's placing his own personal interest over the child's interests. Sadly, many of us make the same mistake, and my own, which follows, is probably all too common.

A Liberal Arts Nerd, Just Like Myself

By the time our adopted son, Thomas, had come to us at the age of six months, we had already had his entire life planned out for him. He would attend the finest private elementary and secondary schools we could afford, go on to the same liberal arts university that both I and his mother had attended, study literature and philosophy and history and the arts, become a teacher, and join the ranks of the rest of us on our quest to transform the world through education.

It sure made sense to me: Who wouldn't want to be a liberal arts nerd, just like myself? What else in life is there to strive for?

Well, Thomas would have none of it. He resisted our efforts to remake him in our own image, instead charting out a course, subconsciously at first, quite deliberately as he matured, that would lead him in an entirely different direction. And we, wanting to be good parents, resisted him, insisting instead that we knew best. But Thomas's will was stronger, and his course prevailed. And we are truly thankful for it.

The mistake we made was a common one. We assumed- remember the barriers?- that Thomas's interests and talents would be the same as ours. Or worse, we assumed that we could fashion his interests and talents for him.

But Thomas is unique, as is each of us, and his interests and talents would emerge from within himself, not from our outside pressure. Thomas would have nothing of the liberal arts. An extremely hard worker who will read voluminously to prepare for a test, he has never "read for pleasure" in his life, and probably never will. His orientation is as far from the liberal arts as one can get: His talents are, instead, entrepreneurial. He can evaluate business opportunities, know instinctively when to make major purchases and when not, choose the best investment strategies, and work extreme hours to accomplish results. He would struggle interminably over a textbook math problem that involves calculating interest on a bank account, but he can determine intuitively the effect of various interest rates on his *own* accounts. Such is the nature of his talent.

Thomas began to blossom when we began to back off. When we dropped our agenda for him, he discovered his own and took flight. When we decided to stop *involving* ourselves in his world and started instead to *show real interest* in his world, the pressure was released and he realized his potential.

Demonstrating Real Interest in Our Children's Interests

Dropping our own agenda for our son was very difficult for us, but once it was dropped a real burden was released as well, a burden for both us and him. In looking back and trying to identify what it was that allowed us to drop our agenda, we have identified two behaviors that were contributory. The first was Thomas's own stubbornness: He knew what he wanted and he went for it, in spite of our failure to comprehend.

But another behavior was our own conscious effort to listen more carefully to what was on his mind. To listen to what he was saying when he would get back from work or school or a movie with friends. To listen to what he was saying when what he was saying was not prompted by our questions. To listen to what came forth from *his* agenda. If you really want to find out what your child's real interests are, observe him when no one is telling him what to do and when you are not actively involved with him.

Our previous attempts to get into Thomas's world, once we grudgingly accepted that he *had* a separate world, were clumsy. We struggled awkwardly, as many parents do, and our attempts at meaningful dialogue followed a pattern that is probably all too familiar:

Dad: "How was school today, Son?"
Thomas: "Fine."
Dad: "So what happened in school today?"

136

Thomas: "Nuthin'"

Dad: "Well, did you have a good day?"

Thomas: "Yeah."

Change occurred when we made the decision to wait for Thomas to comment on his day without our prompting, listen very carefully to that comment, and then engage him in conversation about it. The more he felt that we were sincerely interested in what was going on in his world, the more he would open up . . . and the more interested we actually became in the things that interested him. If communication with your child is a problem, remember this: If he does not respond to your questions, just stop asking the questions and listen to what he *does* say, and then build the conversation around that.

Don't Just Hear; Listen!

Ever since Thomas was old enough to pick up a ball, we would spend some time together, on a daily basis when he was a toddler, maybe weekly during his elementary school years, throwing the ball around. That was the expression we used- "throwing the ball around." In spring and summer, it was a baseball; in fall and winter, a football. In either case, we were "throwing the ball around."

What I never realized during all those years was that for Thomas "throwing the ball around" was a form of communication with his dad. "Throwing the ball around" had very little to do with the mechanics of sport for him; it was all about being with his dad, one on one, and communicating.

It hit home finally when he was in his mid teens and he came to me one Saturday and said, "Hey, Dad, let's go out and throw the ball around." My reply indicated that I had no sense whatsoever of what he was asking me. I had no sense whatsoever that Thomas was saying to me, in his own way: "Dad, you've been ignoring me for some time now and I'd like a little of your time to chat. But I really don't know what to chat about, and if I start talking to you now while you're reading the paper you probably won't listen anyway. So let's go outside and throw the ball around because when we do that you have to pay attention to me- if for no other reason than to avoid getting beaned on the head!"

Not understanding all that and hearing only the words "let's throw the ball around" coming from a fifteen-year-old with plenty of friends, I replied: "Thomas, you don't need me to throw the ball around any more. You're fifteen years old. Go throw the ball around with your friend David." Thomas just walked away.

My reply to Thomas was literally correct- he didn't need me to throw the ball around any more. But that was not what he really wanted. He wanted to be with his dad. And although I heard his words, I wasn't *listening* to him. I never stopped to ask myself, "What could Thomas really be asking me? He has friends to throw the ball around with. Why is he asking me to be with him?" If I had asked- if I had listened, not just heard- I would not have shut him out of my life.

When we hear, we pick up the content. When we listen, we pick up both the content and the context. The content- throwing the ball around- was easy to grasp. The context- a fifteen-year-old who wanted some time with his dad- required a deeper level of attention. It required listening.

Practice listening. Look for the context, not just the content. Tune in to what your children are really saying. Show real interest in them.

Interest Means Respect

When we show real interest in what is going on in another person's world, we are showing that person our deepest respect. When we substitute *our* world for that of the other, we show a lack of respect.

Neil Perry, the central character in the motion picture *Dead Poets' Society,* discovered an interest in the world of the theater. He tried out for and won the lead role in *A Midsummer's Night's Dream* and received the admiration of his fellow students and teachers for his performance. In astonishment, he found himself saying at the end of the performance, "I was good. I was really good." He had found something, the theater, that he truly loved, excelled at, and was determined to pursue further.

But his father would have none of it. He had sent his son to Welton Academy to receive the educational foundation he would need to go on to Harvard and then become a doctor (Dad's agenda), not to dissipate his energies in the theater (Neil's agenda). When his efforts to prevent his son from involving himself in the school drama program failed, he decided to take more forceful action and withdraw him from the school. Neil, deprived of the one thing he really wanted, the one thing that gave him true pleasure, the one thing that provided him an outlet for his new-found talent, ended it all in the tragic climax of the movie.

This is, of course, an extreme reaction to parental control over a young person's life. But it demonstrates clearly, if a bit dramatically, the disrespect that we show when we substitute our own agenda for that of our children.

Billy, twelve and in the seventh grade, is the first born of a family of four. Studies in birth order suggest that first-born children tend to demonstrate qualities of perfectionism. They tend to be over-achievers, and are often overly critical, of self and others. Since their only older role models are parents- unlike any brothers or sisters who follow them, who will have brothers or sisters for older role models-, first borns often develop the perception that they must be perfect, as they perceive their parents to be. To reach that perfection, they tend to push the envelope of their capabilities, become overly critical of their mistakes, and demonstrate impatience with the shortcomings of others.

These perceptions tend to surface in first borns even with no push in that direction from their parents. Unfortunately, Billy's parents actively reinforced those perceptions, communicating very clearly that it was his job to justify them to their neighbors. He was to be perfect, as they were perfect, in all things. See our perfect son. See how he reflects on our own perfection. See what model parents we are. Such was Billy's world, as he perceived it and as his parents actively shaped it.

The problems started early. In fact, they started the very first day of kindergarten. Billy's parents had dressed him to perfection, combed and greased down every last hair, and instructed him, for the umpteenth time, on what they expected of his academic and behavioral performance. He was reminded to sit up straight, to use the right utensil when eating lunch, to avoid slurping his milk, to flush after using the commode, to print his name clearly, to keep his shirt tucked in, to check the shine on his shoes after playing outside, and on and on and on.

When Billy approached the classroom door, five years of anxiety erupted within him. He threw himself to the floor and kicked and screamed with wild abandon. He cried and pleaded and tore at his clothes. He begged his parents to take him home. He simply could not handle that room. The expectations were just too much. Such was Billy's introduction to school.

Billy struggled throughout his elementary school years. His social skills were extremely poor, in spite of the fact (or, perhaps, because of the fact) that he grew up in a very social-conscious and very proper family. He had terrible difficulty getting along with his classmates, appearing to enjoy zeroing in on their weak points and terrorizing them verbally.

He was particularly insensitive to weakness or imperfection. The only teachers he would mind would be the more authoritarian kind. Any teacher who tried to model a more respectful style would be fair game. Respectfulness and gentleness were perceived as indicators of weakness, and Billy hated weakness. As you might guess, Billy spent his elementary school years in near-continuous trouble. He alienated his classmates, he alienated his teachers, and he appeared to even alienate his parents, who would often shift discussion of Billy toward discussion of their other children, who were not experiencing his difficulties.

His parents had great difficulty accepting that Billy's difficulties stemmed from the pressure they had placed on him early in life, and which they continued to place on him. Desirous of having the perfect family, they feared relaxing their grip on Billy, lest he totally rebel. Finally, we were able to convince them that he has already rebelled, and that they need to back off if they expect him to return.

Billy is seventeen now. After four years of family counseling, his parents and teachers are noticing slow but steady progress. His social skills are improving. He is beginning to accept the fact of his own imperfection, and the imperfection of others. But how much was lost in the process!

Billy's parents raised him to be perfect. In counseling, it was revealed that Dad demanded perfection of his wife, and she in turn assumed that it was her responsibility to demand it of the children. The dad was a highly motivated achiever, and he expected the same of those who worked under him- at the office and at the home.

Like Neil Perry's dad, Billy's parents had a chiseled-in-granite plan for Billy. But whereas the plan for Neil was quite specific- he was to go on to Harvard and become a doctor- that for Billy was more general, though none the less demanding- he was to be perfect, in all things. They were not interested in Billy's interests. They were not interested in Billy's world. They were interested, instead, in a pattern, a mold, created from their own minds, and they demanded that Billy fit that pattern. He couldn't do it, so he rebelled.

(Somewhere along the line, Billy would have benefitted from hearing the story of Babe Ruth, whose 714 home runs were scattered among almost twice as many strike outs, a success/failure ratio also matched by slugger Hank Aaron, the man who made baseball history by topping the Babe in both the home run and strike out categories with 755 and 1383 respectively. And no one would call those men failures.)

If demonstrating respect for the uniqueness of each child is
accomplished by showing real interest in their own world, then it
would help to look at some of the many ways that our children can
demonstrate their uniqueness so that we can more effectively enter
that world. Personalities, behavior styles, interests, talents,
intelligence styles, and even birth order are some of the more
dramatic ways through which our children demonstrate their
uniqueness. In the next few sections we will review some of these
areas in order that we might come to know our children's world
better and thereby be more open to showing real interest in it.

Personality and Behavior Styles

About 2500 years ago, a Greek philosopher by the name of
Hippocrates hypothesized that there were four basic personality
styles. He further hypothesized that although each one of us is a

mixture of these basic personality styles, each of us tends to possess a dominant style that affects how we behave more often than not. Hippocrates' four styles have come down to us through the ages as the choleric (dominant, forceful, 'testy'), sanguine (cheery, outgoing, extroverted), phlegmatic (composed, impassive, easy-going), and melancholic (introspective, cautious, moody) styles.

Since Hippocrates, there have been numerous attempts to identify personality and behavior styles. One of the more popular, the Personal Profile System (DiSC model) from the Carlson Learning Company, classifies behavior according to the dominant, influencing, steadiness, and conscientious styles. Focusing on the uniqueness of each individual, the Personal Profile System insists that it does not classify individuals, only behaviors, and encourages users of the profile to personalize it as they go through the process. The result of the process is a fascinating look at individual strengths and weaknesses, goal orientations, motivations, and unique ways to be of service to the organization, family, or community.

It is often argued that approaches to understanding people such as the Personal Profile System contain an internal danger, that of reducing people to types and communicating a deterministic model that denies our uniquely human potential to change and grow. Critics remind us that through our creativity and imagination we are always capable of transcending our present situation, of rewriting our present script, of learning new behaviors and discarding old ones. This is, of course, true, and it is healthy in using any behavior style instrument to be careful to steer clear of that temptation.

But it is also true that there are identifiable and distinct behavior styles that differentiate us. Rudolph Dreikurs, whose *Children: The*

Challenge and other works introduced parents to a new, more respectful approach to parenting, identified four goals of mistaken behavior (power, revenge, attention, and assumed inadequacy) that children demonstrate when they sense that they do not belong. Since goal orientation is strongly related to behavior style, Dreikurs found himself accused from time to time of "putting children in boxes" by labeling them according to their goal. His response: "I'm not putting them in boxes; I'm finding them there."

For whatever reason, we all demonstrate unique and identifiable styles that are descriptive of the behavior that we are most comfortable projecting. By nature, I may be introverted and introspective and enjoy being alone. And although this might accurately *describe* me, it does not *determine* me. If the situation calls for it, I can be out-going and sociable. It may not come to me naturally, but I can do it. But I'd still rather be home alone with a good book.

One way to show real interest in our children is to make the effort to understand their unique behavior style. And we really don't need a personality style assessment instrument to do this. We just need to listen to them. We just need to get into their world.

Do your children need a great deal of alone time, or do they need the continual presence of others? Do they tend to be task oriented, or more people oriented? Do they process their thoughts slowly or quickly? Inwardly or externally? Through reflection or through discussion? Awareness of these questions is the first step to understanding our child's unique behavior style, and the distance from awareness to respect can be short one, if we work at it.

The way we interrelate with others is very much a function of our unique behavior style. Some children will make friends easily; for others, the word 'friends' will be used very restrictively. Some children will be "take-charge" types, leading their classmates in adventure after adventure; others will prefer to follow. Some will be task-oriented, focusing on the job at hand and paying less attention to people needs; still others will be more people-oriented, with the task at hand being placed in a secondary position to the immediate needs of the people involved. In all of this it's good to remember that in interpersonal relationships the Golden Rule doesn't always work. In interpersonal relationships, it is more effective to treat others according to *their* style, not according to our own. Do unto others not as you would have done unto you, but as they would have done unto them.

At a PTA meeting attended by well over five hundred school parents and teachers, a dad in the audience came up to the podium and started talking about a service award that was to be presented. As it turned out, I was to be the recipient. He called me up to the front, and proceeded to speak at length about my supposed accomplishments, with me standing there looking at the floor and praying for the ordeal to be over. This particular individual thrives on public recognition. He would like nothing better than to have been in my position at the time, and so he built it all up just as he would like it built up for him if he were the recipient of the award. He treated me as he would like to be treated. He treated me according to his own behavior style, which is outgoing, extroverted, and social.

But my style is more introverted and private. I like recognition as much as anyone, and, frankly, I want others to know about whatever recognition I might receive, but not by being placed on public display. Come to me privately and tell me that you read about some award I received and you will make my day. But put me on public display and I will pray for an early exit. Treat me as I want to be treated, not as you want to be treated.

In our efforts to get into our children's worlds, let's be careful not to assume that they want to be treated as we do. They may prefer to be left alone when they are down, even though we ourselves may prefer to be with others. Respect that preference. They may prefer just a few good friends, even though we may be friends with everyone in the community. Again, respect that preference. They may prefer private recognition, even though we may prefer public recognition. One more time: Let's respect that preference.

Multiple Intelligences and Talents

One of the healthiest discoveries of recent times is the understanding that there is more to intelligence than that which is measured by standard IQ tests. Two recent books, Daniel Goleman's *Emotional Intelligence* and David Lazear's *Seven Ways of Knowing,* have been particularly instrumental in broadening our understanding of intelligence and opening us up to a greater appreciation and respect for the diversity of talents in our young people, as well as our not-so-young. Our commitment to show real interest in our children's world is strengthened when we open ourselves to the possibility that their intelligence is expressed in different ways from our own. We allow ourselves to see things in them that we would not otherwise be able to see. Further, the more we know about the diversity of intelligences in the world, the better equipped we are to help our children tap into their particular strengths, shore up any relative weaknesses, and become more well-

147

rounded individuals, surely a plus as they progress through the school years.

The pioneering work in the area of recognizing and identifying multiple intelligences was done during the early 1980's by Harvard researcher Howard Gardner, and is most recently popularized by David Lazear who, in *Seven Ways of Knowing,* explores the seven specific intelligences previously identified by his mentor, Gardner. Careful not to close the book on additional intelligences not yet recognized as such, both Gardner and Lazear point out that the identification of seven intelligences is somewhat arbitrary. In fact, at one point Gardner had identified as many as twenty distinct intelligences. But the seven classifications of intelligences that they have arrived at effectively communicate the thesis that intelligence is not one dimensional but is, instead, broad and diverse. The seven classifications are: verbal/linguistic, logical/mathematical, visual/spatial, body/kinesthetic, musical/rhythmic, interpersonal, and intrapersonal. In the following thumbnail descriptions, see if you can identify the particular strengths of your children:

• Verbal/linguistic- the ability to use words and language effectively and creatively in writing, reading, speaking, and listening; the child with strong verbal/linguistic intelligence will excel in activities that require good communications skills, critical thinking, and exchanging ideas.

• Logical/mathematical- the ability to think abstractly, to recognize patterns, and to see connections between separate pieces of information; the child with strong logical/mathematical intelligence will excel in activities that require conceptual organization such as strategic planning, program design, and product development.

• Visual/spatial- the ability to form images and pictures in the mind and to work effectively with patterns, shapes, physical relationships, and colors; the child with strong visual/spatial intelligence will excel in activities that require a talent for aesthetic design, architecture, and the creative arts.

• Body/kinesthetic- the ability to use the body to express emotion (as in dance), to play a game (as in athletics), or to create (as in making a new invention); the child with strong body/kinesthetic intelligence will excel in activities that require physical dexterity such as sports, dance, and mechanics.

• Musical/rhythmic- the ability to recognize and direct rhythmic and tonal patterns in creative ways; the child with strong musical/rhythmic intelligence has the ability to stir the emotions through musical sound (and he's probably tapping his pencil on the table as he's doing his homework!)

• Interpersonal- the ability to deal effectively with others in relationships and communication; the child with strong interpersonal skills will excel in activities that require working with others, being sensitive to others, and leading others; this may well be the most 'useful' intelligence.

• Intrapersonal- the ability to reflect upon the self and understand one's own feelings and emotions; the child with strong intrapersonal intelligence will excel in activities that require thoughtful reflection.

149

Our challenge as parents in reflecting on these seven intelligences is not so much to identify our children's particular strengths (although that is important in fulfilling our commitment to respect their uniqueness), but to raise our own consciousness of the diversity of intelligence so that we might more effectively create a home environment that maximizes the potential for our children to be exposed to that diversity. If these seven intelligences represent the fullness of individual capability, then it would be worthwhile for us to seek ways to expose that fullness to our children. Why narrow their exposure to just two or three of the intelligences (even if those happen to be the ones more appreciated by our culture) if we can expose them to all seven? So in the chart below we will look at each of the intelligences in terms of ways that will allow us to provide opportunities for our children to benefit from experiences that awaken that intelligence in them and raise each to its fullest potential.

Intelligence	Opportunities for Exposure in the Home
Verbal/Linguistic	Reading to your children; listening to them read; encouraging them to keep diaries, journals, or travelogues; writing letters, such as thank-you letters for gifts; telling stories; listening to their stories; being playful with words (jokes, puns, nonsense words)
Logical/Mathematical	Providing toys that involve patterns and shapes; engaging in problem-solving activities and games; encouraging simple math processes during the course of daily

activities (shopping at the grocery store, for example); designing a recycling program for the home

Visual/Spatial	Providing basic building, designing, coloring, painting, and sculpting materials; encouraging child's own decorating of room; creating family calendars and family chores charts
Body/Kinesthetic	Engaging in movement activities such as dancing, roller skating, tumbling, and play-wrestling; playing games that involve movement such as sports activities and dramatic interpretation
Musical/Rhythmic	Playing musical games using hand and body movements along with song ("patty cake," skipping rope, bouncing on the knee while singing); playing musical games that involve humming, whistling, tapping, and other playful sounds; making up playful songs to communicate ideas; playing a wide variety of music in the home
Interpersonal	Practicing effective communication skills, particularly listening, empathizing, and sharing thoughts; doing household activities together as a team; allowing children to speak

for themselves rather than speaking for them; treating children as real people when in conversation with other adults; respecting their feelings, opinions, and moods

Intrapersonal   Respecting, encouraging, and answering child's 'why' questions; engaging in 'what if' activities; modeling self-discipline; encouraging diaries to record emotions, feelings, and thoughts; providing spiritual activities such as meditating and praying

Providing a full range of activities for our children through which we can maximize their exposure to the diversity of intelligences is clearly a tall order. But note that in the recommendations given above, none demands the purchase of expensive materials or the expenditure of special school tuition or the hiring of nannies or any other major material commitment. (And note the absence of any reference to TV!)

What they all do demand is our healthy involvement with our children, an involvement that does not mean "planning their every activity," but, instead, simply being with them and giving them focused attention. If we really want to expose our children to the fullest range of intelligences possible, we just need to get creatively involved with them: read to them, play spatial games with them, build blocks with them, mold clay with them, color with them, sing songs with them, tell stories to them, and respectfully acknowledge their 'why' questions. In doing so we will not only provide the widest possible range of intelligences, but we will be affirming them as very special people who deserve all that we can give them- not of things, but of ourselves.

School-Smart Parenting Tip

Provide a wide range of simple, natural experiences for your children that encompass as many of the intelligences as possible. You will be both expanding their range of interests and increasing the possibility that their own unique talents will be discovered and enhanced.

And they will enter school more open and more receptive to what they will be learning, and more able to benefit from the variety of their school experiences.

Following the insights of Howard Gardner and his disciple David Lazear, Daniel Goleman, in his 1995 best seller *Emotional Intelligence,* argues that our ability to handle our emotions and respond appropriately to them is an 'intelligence' that has for too long gone unappreciated. How many of us know individuals who in spite of a very high level of traditionally-measured intelligence (high scores on the Stanford-Binet Intelligence Scale, SATs in the 1500s, straight 'A's in calculus) nevertheless appear to be unsuccessful in getting ahead in the "real world"? These folks may be strong in verbal and mathematical intelligence, but they are weak, argues Goleman, in emotional intelligence.

Goleman identifies five components of emotional intelligence.

Once again, try to identify the particular strengths of your children as we briefly review these qualities:

• Being aware of your own emotions- the ability to self-assess or identify and accept our feelings (I am angry because Robert took my ball.)

• Being able to manage your emotions- the ability to make appropriate choices in response to our feelings (I have choices in how I respond to Robert for taking my ball; I can choose to hit him, or I can go tell the teacher, or I can talk to him, or . . .)

• Being able to motivate yourself- the ability to place needs over wants to accomplish what needs to be accomplished (I'd rather just hit Robert, but that is not the right thing to do so I will go and talk to him instead.)

• Recognizing emotions in others- the ability to read the feedback that comes to us from others (I can see that Robert was angry with me for not playing with him and maybe that's why he took my ball.)

• Handling relationships- the ability to respond effectively to emotions in others (Maybe if I play with Robert he will be happy and not angry with me anymore.)

Probably the most effective ways to teach these components of emotional intelligence is, first, to model them in our own lives, and, second, to provide specific real life opportunities for our children to practice them in their lives. The chart below offers specific suggestions of how we might accomplish this:

Emotion	Opportunities for Role Modeling and Practice
Awareness	Taking ownership of our own emotions through "I" statements ("I am angry about the way you left the bathroom, because it was just cleaned and now there is water all over the floor."); allowing and respecting the child's emotions through empathy ("I can understand being afraid of the dark. I can remember being afraid of the dark too.")
Managing Emotions	Waiting before responding when angry; using time out, both for ourselves and for our children; asking "What else could you have done . . . ?" instead of "Why did you do that?"
Motivation	Sharing personal goals with your children; helping them break down long-term goals into smaller, manageable parts; giving allowances to encourage opportunities for them to make their own choices in buying things; avoiding rescuing; allowing natural consequences; applying logical consequences
Recognizing	Respecting emotions in others ("Your mother

Emotions	is very upset right now because of the mess in the bathroom. This is not the time to ask her when dinner will be ready."); avoiding attempts to forcefully change emotions ("Stop crying right now and enjoy the movie with the rest of the family.")
Handling Relationships	Responding respectfully to others' emotions by actively acknowledging them ("Since Mom is so upset about the way the bathroom was left, why don't we start the dinner for her."); avoiding the temptation to problem solve for another or "should have" for another ("You ruined your new dress because you pressed down too hard with the iron. What you should have done is . . .")

When we take ownership of our feelings through "I" statements, practice time out, defer gratification, and acknowledge and respond effectively to others' emotions, we model emotional intelligence for our children and provide opportunities for them to grow in their ability to work more effectively with others.

Showing real interest in our children must include an openness, appreciation, and respect for the different ways that they express their intelligence. This can be demonstrated in many ways. In a touching scene from the pilot movie that introduced the television series *The Waltons,* John, the father, returns home on Christmas Eve with small gifts for each of the children. In presenting his gift to John-Boy, a sensitive child who loved to write, John confessed that although he couldn't understand his son's love for writing he bought him this gift to support his efforts. The gift- Big Chief writing tablets- was the last thing that the father would want for himself, but the best gift that John-Boy could receive. John may not have understood his son's verbal/linguistic intelligence, but he respected it enough to give him a gift that would provide him an outlet for that talent. (Unlike the parents of the young man in *Dead Poets' Society* who received a desk set- the same one- every year for his birthday.)

When we appreciate that each child is talented and gifted in his own unique way and make efforts to understand the unique mode of intelligence that each of our children possesses, we demonstrate respect for them. And we give concrete expression to that respect when the gifts we give them on special occasions reflect their (not our) talents, when we allow them to organize their world (particularly their room) to reflect their own interests, and when we engage them in conversation about their interests. In doing so, we provide them the opportunity to more fully understand their strengths as well as an incentive to open up to ours.

All that has been said above about exposing our children to the multiple intelligences and opportunities to develop their emotional intelligence is even more important in the early years of life. If we place our young children in front of the television all day they will become passive participants in their world. If we instead give them opportunities to fashion their world with blocks and boxes and string and clay, make the effort to provide a natural home environment that is diverse and broad, and model emotional maturity, all when they are very young, they will approach their school years with the habit of active involvement, a wide diversity of interests, and an emotional maturity that will surely serve them well.

High Expectations

What about high expectations? Is it not true that study after study has demonstrated that a teacher's or parent's high expectations of a child's potential will positively affect his achievement? If so, how does this square with our need to respect each child's uniqueness and avoid the temptation to hold them up in comparison to a model of success that we have in our minds, rather than to encourage them to fulfill their own unique potential?

The classic study on the effect of high expectations on students took place in 1968 under Harvard professors Robert Rosenthal and Lenore Jacobsen. Taking two similar groups of elementary school children, labeling one group as gifted (using their locker numbers, which were numbered in the 120's, to assign them fake IQ scores) and the other group as average, Rosenthal and Jacobsen discovered that the children labeled as gifted did in fact excel in school, regardless of their actual IQ score. They noticed that the teachers of the students labeled as gifted gave them more opportunities to answer questions and more time to answer them in, addressed them more often by name, and stepped closer to and touched them more often. The teachers' high expectations of the students affected the way they were treated and the way they performed in response to that treatment- powerful information for teachers and parents alike.

More recently, the cause of high expectations has been celebrated by the motion picture *Stand and Deliver,* the story of East Los Angeles high school math teacher Jaime Escalante, who galvanized a group of ghetto kids into becoming advanced placement calculus scholars. In a biography that followed the success of the motion picture, *Escalante: The Best Teacher in America* by Jay Mathews, the story is told of Henry Gradillas, Garfield High School biology teacher during the 1970's and role model for Escalante himself. Gradillas, troubled by the absence of positive expectations among many of his fellow teachers and many of the students, quietly embarked on an experiment to test out the power of high expectations. Two basic biology classes, containing similar students divided randomly, were told, in the one case, that they were college material with much potential and, in the other case, that they were lazy and there was little hope for them. Giving more difficult tests and more homework to the first group and just the minimum to the second, his expectations proved true . . . in both cases. During the first quarter, the first group lived up to his expectations by mastering a college-level biology test; the second lived down to his expectations by producing only one 'A,' with 30% of the class getting 'D's and 'F's. Doing his best to salvage the rest of the year by communicating high expectations for both, Gradillas never could undo the damage he had done to the second group.

High expectations became the rallying cry for Jaime Escalante, and his success, and the success of so many others who have held high expectations for their students, demonstrates its importance. When based on respect for the potential of young people, high expectations can have profound, positive effects. Showing real interest in our children's world must include our high expectations for their success.

But there are two cautions that must be expressed here. One, we need to avoid the temptation to expect right now what we see as a long-term goal. If we expect our children to demonstrate at 8:00 in the morning on September 1 the complete range of academic and behavioral outcomes expected upon completion of the grade in June, we are doing a disservice to them. Progress comes in steps, sometimes very small steps, and as long as we can see that effort is being made toward that progress, and continue encouraging our children along the way, we are effectively communicating high expectations.

And second, unrealistic expectations that do not respect the specific talents and capabilities of our children may only result in discouragement. I can practice hitting baseballs twelve hours a day, seven days a week, for a full year, and at the end of that year I will be far more proficient than I was before I started. And the high expectations of my coach will go a long way toward encouraging me and supporting me as I gain confidence to keep on trying.

But no matter how much I might practice and no matter how high the expectations of my coach, I will never be able to connect with a Nolan Ryan fast ball with a proficiency that would gain the attention of even the most forgiving baseball scout. I simply do not have that potential because I was not gifted with that talent- Gardner's body/kinesthetic intelligence-, and adults who tell me that I can do anything I want in life if I just keep trying are doing me a disservice. I have a range of abilities in any number of areas, and practice, commitment, and high expectations will enable me to test the outer limits of those ranges. And I will be a better and more complete person because of it. But my ranges are not your ranges, and the high expectations of others must respect that.

We do a disservice to our children if we communicate to them that our high expectations for them demand that they excel in these specific areas and in these specific ways, right now. Our challenge is to be open to our children's unique talents, intelligences, interests, and hobbies, communicate to them our highest expectations for their efforts, and acknowledge the accomplishments that result from their efforts.

The Child's Room: A Place of His Own

One very important area in which we can communicate to our children that their uniqueness is worthy of our respect is the degree to which we allow the child to see his room as *his* room, which includes the issue of what requirements we will make for the care and cleanliness of that room. To the degree to which a child sees his room as *his* room, he will be more willing to respect it and work in it. And he will appreciate having a place of his own, a place that is his domain and his responsibility.

I believe strongly that we should allow the child's room to be his room: a place to decorate as he wishes, a place to enjoy his own music, a place of privacy that we should not, under normal circumstances, enter against his wishes. There are limits to all this, of course- after all, the child's room is part of our house, which we pay for every month and which we must maintain at a certain level of care and cleanliness. And the child is part of a larger family with responsibilities to that larger family.

But the limits that we set should be done not to control the child but to teach respect for the *whole* family. A child should not be allowed to punch holes in the walls, for example, as this will devalue the house. He should not be allowed to play music that can be heard in the next county, because this negatively impacts the rest of the family, not to mention the neighbors. And he should not be allowed to go weeks recycling dirty clothes as this will make life miserable for anyone who comes in contact with him. (One of the skills we should teach our children at the earliest possible time is taking care of their own clothes. Even elementary school age children are perfectly capable of differentiating between white clothes and colored clothes, warm water and cold water, half loads and full loads. And the operation of washing machines and dryers is about as non-technical as it can be. If our children are capable of programing our VCRs and figuring out all the intricacies of the family computer, they are certainly capable of doing their own wash. Oh, and by the way, so is Dad.)

All of this applies just as well in situations where children have to share bedrooms. Children who share bedrooms have the opportunity to learn cooperation skills as they work out the issues of space, decorating, privacy, cleanliness, noise level, etc., and we parents are called upon to allow them to work them out, with as little interference as possible.

Regarding neatness and cleanliness, just how concerned should we be about the state of our children's rooms? And just how concerned should we be that our children have a place where they can test out their own organizational skills, a place they can decorate according to their own styles, a place that is comfortable for them, a place of their own?

Where is the line separating our dual desires for neatness, cleanliness, and 'showability,' on the one hand, and individuality, creativity, and personal ownership, on the other? What responsibilities should our children be given regarding their own rooms? And what rights should they have?

These do not look like easy questions, but they might be easier to approach than we would think. A good litmus test for evaluating our approach to the question of our child's room might be this: Are the decisions we are making being made for our child's benefit . . . or for our own? Are we looking out more for our own interest- that we look good to the neighbors, that we fulfill our need for perfection (or someone else's need for perfection), that we control every aspect of our children's lives-, or are we looking out for the child's best interests- his need to learn organizational skills, his need to learn responsibility for his own things, his need for privacy?

Perhaps the best question to ask is this: Exactly what am I not comfortable allowing? Books not lined up evenly on the bookshelf?

An unmade bed? Clothes on the floor? Peanut butter sandwiches under the bed? Clearly there is wide variation here- so just what am I not comfortable allowing?

A helpful rule of thumb might be this: When dealing with a child's room, allow the child more freedom than you would allow for the rest of the house. Maybe you can't stand having your own bed left unmade. But is it that important that your children make theirs everyday? If it is, then make that your rule. But if not, then establish another requirement- beds made once a week, or only when company is coming. (A friend of mine who works in parent education puts it very simply to those who take her classes: You don't like the way your child's room looks? Close the door!)

In short, let's allow our children a little more freedom in their own little piece of the world. Let's give them space to demonstrate their own personality. Let's give them a safe place to test out their organizational skills. Let's model respect for privacy by practicing it as it affects their own room.

Self-Esteem Revisited

Carl was a high school football star and successful college athlete who lived for the day his own young son, Trent, would be old enough to play community sports. At age five, Trent was enrolled in a soccer program and told by Dad that this was just warm-up for football, which would come later and in which he would be expected to become the captain of the team. At six, Trent was signed up for T-ball, and again reminded that this was only a dress rehearsal for the really big day when he would don a football uniform and lead his teammates on the field as their captain.

164

Basketball and hockey were introduced later with the same reminders- this was just practice for the real sport, football, in which you will be the captain of the team.

Trent was as excited and filled with anticipation as was his father when the football season opened during his first year of eligibility, grade six at eleven years old. This was the sport of sports, the game *par excellence,* and he was going to play and become the team captain.

Trent didn't become the team captain that first year- the football program he had entered was a three-year program, ending at grade eight, and the team captain had always been an eighth grader. But still, Trent thought it wasn't quite right, that it was somehow unfair that he wasn't chosen captain that year. Had not his father raised him to be captain?

He didn't make captain the second year either. A seventh grader then, Trent was "passed over" (his perception) for an eighth grader. When the captain's name was announced, Trent stomped out of the locker room, furious, resulting in discipline from his coach. His dad was also furious that he was passed over for captain: " . . . just because you're in the seventh grade. You should be captain, and the coach knows it. This isn't fair to have to wait another year."

By the time eighth grade rolled around, Trent and his dad had almost forgiven the coach for passing him over as captain. All would be completely forgiven when Trent was announced as captain this year and the slight of last year was rectified. But it didn't happen. Another child was chosen as captain. And Dad pulled Trent off the team, accusing the coach of "destroying my son's self-esteem" and threatening a law suit. But who was it that set the child up for eventual failure?

(I would add that if you think the above story is a bit extreme, well then you haven't been around community or school sports enough yet. In conversation about legal issues with a local superintendent of schools, I once asked what the most frequent cause of parent-initiated litigation was. Her reply: Parents whose daughters did not make the cheerleading team. Remember the story from Texas about the woman accused of conspiring to kill the mother of a cheerleader competitor, so that the competitor would be too distracted to compete successfully against her own daughter? The intensity of emotions is all too real here.)

The importance of healthy self-esteem cannot be over-estimated. But what it is, where it comes from, and what are its limitations are often overlooked. When Trent's father threatened a law suit against the coach for damaging his son's self-esteem, he clearly indicated a very narrow understanding of the nature, source, and limits of that important feeling. Self-esteem is not arrogance; it is, instead, the feeling that I am worthy of dignity and respect, not because of anything I have done or not done, but just because I am. It does not come to us from the praise from others, well meaning though it may be, or from the gold stars that teachers place on our papers. It comes through experiences we have, both positive experiences and negative experiences, through which we learn that we are capable, significant persons who can make choices that influence our lives. And it is not without limitations. Recycling an old saying, it might not be too simplistic to say that your self-esteem ends where my self-esteem begins. If my self-esteem encourages me to go out into the world with confidence and be of service to others, it is a very valuable thing indeed. If it leads me to believe and act in a manner that suggests that the entire world revolves around my every want and need, then it is harmful.

Several years ago, a new mayor of New York City was inaugurated in a much-publicized, media-highlighted, and, ultimately, very embarrassing ceremony. With his ten-year-old son standing next to him, the new mayor began his inauguration speech. To the embarrassment of all (except, so it appeared, to the mayor himself) and to the delight of the late night talk shows that satirized the event during subsequent weeks, the young son proceeded to mimic his father's words, mug the camera, and gesture theatrically, all to a national television audience.

The boy behaved as someone who was raised to believe that his wants and needs predominate over everything else. He behaved, in fact, as someone whose self-esteem is so high that the needs of the rest of the world- in that case, solemnity and formality, not to mention plain good manners- just don't count. For years we have been told that self-esteem is the most important issue in parenting, that all we need to focus on is raising our children's self-esteem and everything else will work out just fine. But if our current understanding of self-esteem doesn't translate to respect for the needs of others, then the issue of self-esteem is in need of review.

And review it is finally receiving. Thanks to critical thinkers like Alfie Kohn, author of *Punished by Rewards: The Trouble with Gold Stars, Incentive Plans, A's, Praise, and Other Bribes,* the whole self-esteem movement is being subjected to closer inspection. In a December 1994 article in the professional education journal *Kappan,* Kohn summarizes his concern about the direction the self-esteem movement has taken in these jarringly honest words:

"*I'm* special, *I'm* important, here's how *I* feel about things. The whole enterprise could be said to encourage a self-absorption bordering on narcissism."

Those schooled in the "individual" psychology of Alfred Adler and the parenting insights of Rudolph Dreikurs, Stephen Glenn, Jane Nelsen, and Alfie Kohn have long questioned the direction of the self-esteem movement. Two concerns are of particular note regarding the directions that the movement has taken. The first, identified by Kohn in the above quote, concerns the egocentric nature of the vocabulary of self-esteem. *I'm* special; *I'm* important. How important is it that we reinforce this with our children and students?, Kohn asks. Would it not be healthier to teach that we are *all* special, we are *all* important? Of course, both concepts are important. Perhaps the central question is: Are we de-emphasizing the latter in our enthusiasm to promote the former? The examples of the coach's son and the new mayor's son might suggest that we are.

The second concern, identified by many commentators on the issue, revolves around the *source* of self-esteem: Is it primarily achieved from without, or from within? Is it the result of what others say to us and do for us, or is it the result of experiences that we have had, that we have reflected upon, and that we have, consequently, learned from? And if it is the latter, what role should we adults play in providing activities, opportunities, and challenges for our young people through which they can experience a healthy level of self-esteem? And what does it say about just letting go and allowing our children to experience discomfort and even failure, so that they can then learn from that, build a better plan, and discover their own ability to overcome difficulty?

Kohn and others argue that if we really want to help our children

168

feel good about themselves, we should be sure to always treat them with respect, rather than showering them with praise. After all, what does the word 'esteem' mean? It is simply a synonym for 'respect.' So self-esteem is really nothing more than self-respect. And just as we teach responsibility by giving our children responsibilities, we teach self-respect by giving our children respect. Rather that worrying so much about self-esteem all we really need to do is treat people- children and adults alike- with respect. A challenge worth considering . . . and undertaking.

School-Smart Parenting Tip

To promote healthy self-esteem, treat your children with esteem, i.e., with respect. When they experience respect from others, their own self-respect is enhanced.

And they will go to school both feeling respected themselves and being respectful to those they come in contact with, adults and children alike.

Birth Order

In *The Birth Order Book,* author Kevin Leman relates the following statistics about first borns:

- of the first twenty-three astronauts sent into outer space, twenty-one were first borns

• all seven astronauts in the original Mercury program were first borns

• more than half the United States presidents were first borns

• first borns are overrepresented among *Who's Who in America* and *American Men and Women of Science,* as well as among Rhodes scholars and university professors

Get the picture? First borns tend to be highly motivated to achieve. They tend to be analytical, organized, and precise, and they thrive on structure and order. The first-born child is likely to spend hours sorting baseball cards, meticulously furnishing a doll house, playing school (with the first born being the teacher and her friends being the students), organizing stamp and coin collections, strategically positioning the latest action figures around the room, bossing all the other children in the neighborhood, and generally behaving more adult-like than the other children in the family. Why?

The bottom line is that children tend to develop according to the perception they have of their parents' expectations and treatment of them . . . and/or their older siblings expectations and treatment of them. And birth order is a major factor in those expectations and treatment. The first born tends to get a lot of adult attention, and because he is the first born a lot is expected of him. He is the child who is expected to justify the parents before the world. And his parents are his only models. The first born perceives this and responds accordingly.

The second born, particularly so if of the same sex as the first born, perceives very different expectations from the parents. Even though the parents may expect the same of the second born as of the first born, the second born tends to perceive something very different. He perceives that the first born has carved out a little niche for himself, the niche of the little adult who does everything right and whose first tooth and first step and first words and first smile are all dutifully celebrated, communicated, and recorded for posterity by the parents. (And whose first drawings are all publicly displayed on the fridge.)

If the second born is to achieve significance in this family, he will need to find it somewhere other than the places the first born found it. His first tooth, step, words, smile, and drawings will be far less significant than his older bother's. So he must look for another way to be noticed, and he may find it in rebellion. If the first born was Mr. Do-Whatever-Mom-and-Dad-Want (because they will clap and celebrate and call all the aunts and uncles when they do), then the second born may try to do whatever Mom and Dad don't want, to get the attention that would otherwise be denied by following the same pattern as the first born. After all, doing whatever Mom and Dad want, having already been done by the first born, is no longer any big deal.

Let's say along comes a third son. Third son has two older siblings before him as role models for his own development. He perceives that they are very different, if for no other reason than that they are always fighting. And he notices that they are fighting with each other, not with him. So, he concludes, my role must be that of the peacemaker, the mediator. My role in this family is to bring peace between my older brothers.

Let's continue this not-so-hypothetical birth order picture a little further. One year after third born son comes a daughter- the first born daughter. First born daughter has three older brothers ahead of her. First born daughter must fight to survive. First born daughter must use her wits and her words and her strength of character if she is to fend off the buffets of her older siblings. And first born daughter has no time to become privileged only daughter or taken-care-of last born because two years later comes . . .

Second born daughter. Second born daughter enters a home rapidly approaching chaos. First born son and second born son are in constant conflict. Third born son is running around trying to mediate between them. First born daughter is becoming toughened and hardened and just a little bossy as she learns various ways to fend off her brothers' criticisms, insults, and bullying. For second born daughter, the path is clear. Her role is to mediate this mess. Her role is to bring peace. Her role is to cry out, in the midst of all this turmoil, Can't we all just love each other? It is no surprise that second born daughter is best friends with third born son, the first family mediator, the role model of mediators.

Second born daughter, fifth born in the family, didn't have long to savor any unique status she may have enjoyed as the baby. This would be reserved for another daughter, number eight in the family. But before number eight, there came . . . fourth born son, first born after two daughters and three much older brothers, and then fifth born son. And then, finally, the baby, who learned that she could get everyone else to do everything for her if she just turned on the charm.

Like behavior styles and intelligence styles, birth order does not define, but it does describe. First borns and only borns do tend to be leaders, middle children do tend to be mediators, and last born do tend to be charmers. Our role as parents is to recognize the qualities our children are likely to demonstrate as a result of their birth order, maximize the positive aspects of those qualities, and assist them in compensating for any of the negative aspects. Our children are not all the same- You really didn't need to have that pointed out again, did you?- but we often treat them as though they are. The challenge is to treat them all fairly but not necessarily the same, recognizing that each child has different needs. The chart below offers some specific examples of things we can do to accomplish that:

Birth Order	Parenting Opportunities
First Born	Encourage and provide opportunities for her to be with her own age group; share your own imperfections with her; avoid "fixing" her jobs (straightening out the covers on the bed she just made, for example); be a "good finder" by focusing on what she did right and minimizing what she did wrong; allow some special privileges to compensate for the special responsibilities she will have; remember to give her one-on-one time, especially when that second child comes along
Second Child	Accept the differences of the second child; be attuned to different interests, talents, and needs; recognize and acknowledge his

'firsts'; avoid comparisons, avoid comparisons, avoid comparisons; give one-on-one time

Middle Child	Be attuned to the middle child's need to be seen as someone special; avoid overdoing the hand-me-downs; be sure to continue whatever activities you engaged in for the older children (baby pictures, photo albums, drawings posted on the refrigerator, music lessons, etc.); provide special responsibilities and privileges; give one-on-one time
Last Born	Avoid "doing for" and discourage the older children from "doing for"; be especially attuned to providing chores and responsibilities around the house and enforcing family rules; recognize accomplishments; maintain the photo album and post those drawings; give one-on-one time

The more we understand about birth order, the more prepared we are to recognize the behaviors that tend to be associated with each position in the family, and the more prepared we will be to help our children maximize their strengths and minimize their weaknesses.

"Is my child ready for school?"

The law says that our children are eligible to enter kindergarten when they are five years old by September 1 (or whatever the date is in your state). But to be eligible is not necessarily to be ready. And readiness does not have a specific time table.

Readiness is best determined developmentally rather than chronologically. Just as no two of our children take their first steps at the same age, no two of them will be developmentally ready for schooling at exactly the same time. Unfortunately, we often expect them to be ready just because they have turned five, but that is not necessarily the case. So how does the parent know if the child should go to kindergarten, or, instead, stay home for another year of maturation?

Pediatricians, teachers, school counselors, and your own experience can all help here. But there are also some specific clues. If you have concerns that your child may not be ready for kindergarten, use this checklist as a guide:

[ ] Is she comfortable being away from home and her parents for several hours each day?

[ ] Can she take care of her bathroom and hygiene responsibilities?

[ ] Can she express herself- her needs, her concerns, her ideas, her feelings- to other adults and children?

175

[ ] Has she demonstrated the ability to try new things and engage in new activities without undue fear?

[ ] Can she handle her emotions well?

[ ] Can she work well with other children her own age?

[ ] Can she work independently?

[ ] Does she take care of her belongings?

[ ] Does she respect the belongings of others?

[ ] Can she do simple drawings that are recognizable?

[ ] Is her physical coordination in line with other children her age?

[ ] Does pencil control result in firm strokes or wobbly strokes?

(And one question that is *not* a reliable indicator of readiness: Does she demonstrate advanced verbal skills? Demonstrating advanced verbal skills, which is common for first borns, is more an indicator that the child is surrounded more by adults than by other children. Remember that first-born children have only Mom and Dad for models, including models for their verbal skills.)

If your discussion with your pediatrician, teachers and counselors, your own experience and wisdom, and the checklist above lead you to have doubts about your child's readiness, it's probably better that you wait a year. When in doubt, keep her out. There is plenty of time to savor all of life's experiences, and a year held out for developmental readiness will not set anyone back. But pushing a child before she is ready may cause frustrations throughout her school years- continuing lower achievement, feelings of inadequacy, not "fitting in," etc.-, so consider all the above before enrolling your child in kindergarten. It is a very important first decision for parents.

School-Smart Parenting Tip

Avoid the temptation to rush your child. Look seriously at
the readiness question, and if in doubt, keep her out.

That extra year will allow for developmental readiness
and maximize her potential for getting the most
from her school experiences.

Clearly, there is a lot to the issue of showing real interest in our children's world. Perhaps the best way to sum it all up is to emphasize once again that each of our children really is unique. Each of our children really does have a world that is distinct from our own, and from his siblings. And if we recognize that, and support that, we will assist our children in the development of their full potential, and they will begin their school years more excited and more enthusiastic about the new things they will be adding to their growing repertoire of interests and talents.

CHAPTER 6

EMOTIONAL STABILITY:
PROVIDING A SAFE HAVEN IN THE HOME

The wild things roared their terrible roars
and gnashed their terrible teeth
and rolled their terrible eyes and showed their terrible claws
but Max stepped into his private boat and waved good-bye
and sailed back over a year
and in and out of weeks
and through a day
and into the night of his very own room
where he found his supper waiting for him
and it was still hot.

-Where the Wild Things Are

The third behavior that I have found to increase the potential for success and happiness in school is the concerted effort by all family members, but particularly Mom and Dad, to provide emotional stability in the home. When we strive for a home environment characterized by emotional stability, we create a safe and supportive oasis within which our children can test out their strengths and weaknesses, allowing them to build confidence for the school years.

And we minimize the probability of our children's schooling being burdened with the baggage that results from emotional instability in the family.

An October 1993 issue of *USA Today* featured an article describing a survey of adolescents designed to determine the factors that led to success in school. According to the survey, the one factor that correlated most directly with high achievement and self-esteem was not socio-economic status, not race or ethnicity, not whether the school was public or private, nor whether it was located in an affluent neighborhood or in a poor neighborhood, not family make-up, indeed, not any of the factors we readily and carelessly assume to be predictive of success. The one factor that did correlate most directly with achievement in school was whether or not the family sat down to eat dinner together on a regular basis.

And in a study undertaken in 1995 by the publishers of *Who's Who Among American High School Seniors,* the 1993 findings reported in *USA Today* were confirmed. Based on responses from 3351 teenagers, it was revealed that those who regularly share meals with their families are three times more likely to say that their home life is happy and that their relationship with their parents is close.

Sitting down with the family and eating dinner together on a regular basis! What a wonderful advantage for us parents! Teachers can't do that with their students (although regular class meetings might produce many benefits of that experience). But we parents can do it, thereby providing our children with a safe, comfortable, repeatable setting in which they can experience community and develop as healthy young people.

I was giving a presentation not long ago on the subject of raising children for success and happiness in school, when a young mom, the oldest of whose three children would be starting school within a few months, interrupted my comments with the direct challenge: "OK, so just what do I need to do to ensure that my children will be successful in school?" I replied: "Do you really want to know?" "Yes," she shot back, "enough of all this introductory stuff. Just tell me what I need to do." I answered her: "Well, if you really want your children to experience success and happiness in school . . . "- and then I dramatically paused and scanned the audience, making eye contact with as many as I could- " . . . what you really need to do is sit down with them and eat dinner together on a regular basis."

She did not hide her disappointment, but I let the answer hang in the air nonetheless. Finally, she said, with undisguised frustration: "Sit down and eat dinner together??? That's what I drove all the way out here today to hear?" And then I did what experienced speakers do when challenged by an audience participant: I involved the whole audience in problem solving by throwing the issue out to them and challenging them to come up with reasons why sitting down together for dinner would impact a child's emotional stability, thereby leading to success in school. With the audience involved, we were soon able to fill in the details of the picture with a broader perspective on the importance of providing a home environment characterized by emotional stability.

I did not do that to frustrate the questioner, although she probably felt otherwise. I did it to prolong the point, thereby giving it greater emphasis, hoping it would remain with the listeners long after other points made during the presentation were forgotten. In our fast-paced, over-involved, over-scheduled, stress-filled world, there are truly few things better that we can provide for our children than

180

thirty to forty-five minutes together with them- TV off and telephone recorder on- sitting around the dinner table passing the potatoes and sharing thoughts and concerns about the day.

The Influence of Family Life on the Child

The dinner table may be the perfect metaphor for the renewal of family life, which I believe to be absolutely critical to the improvement of our schools. I once heard a speaker, a hardened man who had spent a great deal of his life in prison ministry, talk about the death of the American family. His statistics were chilling: So many more fatherless homes, so many more unwed pregnant teenagers, so many more cases of spousal abuse, so many more cases of child abuse, and on and on. It was a gloomy picture. But his prescription was even gloomier: The American family is dead, and we need to provide other models to replace it; the churches, community organizations, and the local, state, and federal governments must step up to the plate and offer themselves as alternatives to the now-deceased American family.

I could not resist the opportunity to challenge his prescription. I think I began my response by thanking him for his presentation and recognizing a few good points he had made- I hope I did, anyway!-, but after that the gloves came off and I was swinging with both fists. There can be no alternative to the American family, I said. Not the churches, not community organizations, and not- God help us!- the government! (I think I was standing up at this point.) I have seen the American family, and it is alive and well, sitting down together around the dinner table sharing their joys and frustrations and passing the potatoes! There is hope for America!

I sat back down. The speaker looked at me, hesitated, and said, I think: "Thank you for sharing." Others in the audience started moving away from me, very discreetly. And I looked around for the nearest exit.

As humorous as that is, the point remains: There is no alternative to the American family, which of all the institutions that affect us has the greatest influence on the child, and we need to focus our attention there if we are going to save our schools . . . and our children.

Just how important is the influence of the family on the child? Dr. Kevin Leman, who popularized Alfred Adler's theories on birth order and the effects it has on a child's perception of his role in the family in *The Birth Order Book,* argues forcefully that a child's family exerts more influence on him than any other system, organization, institution, or even experience that he might have in life. And as the world out there becomes more and more hectic and fast-paced, more and more confusing and technologically overpowering, more and more threatening, the potential influence of the family is ever increasing. When all else is confusing and confounding, the family at home remains the one true constant that can be counted on to be there . . . around the table eating dinner together, sharing the experiences of the day, listening to each others' joys and frustrations, passing the potatoes.

The Family Dinner

Sitting around the table eating dinner together- what a simple prescription, so simple we are tempted to minimize its importance. But it would be a serious mistake to do so. Schedule an hour, if possible, for the family dinner. Avoid the temptation to run from the table as soon as the dishes are cleared. Leave the TV off. (According to a survey reported in *National Times*, September 1995, 66% of Americans regularly eat dinner while watching TV. So much for dinner time communication.) Let the telephone recorder pick up all those irresistible offers for new credit cards and alternative long distance services and opportunities to contribute to your favorite charity.

And for those families for whom regular dinner together is an impossibility- conflicting work schedules, soccer practices, meetings- decide on at least one or two nights a week that will be kept free from outside distractions and make them special dinner times. Even if only once a week, that special dinner time together can go a long way to providing emotional stability in the family. Some families I have met through my parenting courses who find themselves limited to that one night a week have made a commitment to make of that one night something very special by eating at the formal dinner table, with the guests-only dinnerware, a few candles burning, soft music in the background, and a full meal served leisurely.

The key is to use the family meal as an opportunity for bringing all members of the family together in a relaxed setting with as few distractions as possible. By doing so, we communicate to our family members that they are more important than television, more important than outside schedules, more important than the person on the other end of the telephone.

Of course, as our children grow up and peers become a larger and larger part of their world, they may not want to linger at the table as long as we parents would like. That's OK. Let them go ahead and leave early. Show understanding for their developing personhood.

But- most important!- stay at the table with the other family members for the full meal time and keep the family dinner going. Nothing will provider a safer and more secure harbor for our teenagers than knowing that when they *do* wish to linger with us for the full meal- and they will from time to time- that we are still there, sitting around the table, passing the potatoes.

Family Night

Dad's job keeps him working late four nights a week, Monday through Thursday. Mom has part-time work outside the home, a full carpool schedule before and after, and the cooking to do at the end of the day. (The other family chores are divided as equally as possible among all family members; this family has already read Chapter 4.) Friday night is reserved for Mom and Dad together, and on Saturday nights the kids get involved with their friends on a fairly regular basis. So Sunday is reserved as the one night the family can eat together. It is also reserved as family night.

For many families, family night is an extension of the family meal. Family night simply means one night set aside weekly for the family to be present to one another for an extended period of time playing games, telling stories, reading to each other, making a dessert together, doing projects together, planning outings and vacations, etc. Like the family meal, the scheduled family night is simply one more opportunity to communicate to our children that they are worth our time and attention, that they are more important than all the distractions that our world places before us.

Family nights can be enhanced by allowing the children to choose the activity, by ensuring some variation in the activities, and by throwing in surprises from time to time (a trip to an ice cream shop after the activity, for example). The key is to schedule it and stick with it, like the family meal. And when the teenagers start drifting away, keep on doing it anyway- they will drift back, and when they do they will appreciate that little oasis you have continued to provide on family night.

One final note: Don't forget one-on-one time with the children. As positive an experience as it is to have the entire family together, there is something extra special about taking the time for each child individually. Few interactions more effectively promote the perception that you are an important member of a community than when the head of that community, in this case Mom or Dad, seeks you out for special attention. Most people can vividly remember times when they were young and when they had one of their parent's undivided attention. It's a powerful communicator of significance, one worth making the time for.

The Family Meeting

The weekly family meeting, a structured and somewhat formal opportunity for the family to get together and communicate, might well be the single most effective means of ensuring that all family members will be affirmed as significant, contributing members of the household. The family meeting allows each family member, children as well as adults, to participate in family decision making. It provides an opportunity for sharing both joys and disappointments, for giving compliments and thanks, for speaking and for listening. And it provides a forum for working out difficulties, distributing responsibility for chores, discussing changes in family routines, and planning for activities and vacations.

The mechanics of the family meeting need not be complicated. Simply stated, it is a weekly meeting attended by all family members to share interests and concerns and discuss family issues. Many families provide an agenda in advance, on which each family member can write down items for discussion. This agenda could be a sheet of paper posted on the refrigerator, a shoe box with a slot cut in the top, or any other convenient means to allow for the writing down items of concern. Other families simply give each member a chance to speak, without a formal agenda. In any case, every family member who wishes to do so should be allowed time to contribute.

The setting for the family meeting might take a format similar to the following:

• A chairperson is appointed to keep the meeting on task. If possible, each family member should have a turn at being chairperson.

• Each family member is encouraged to share one positive thing that has happened to them during the past week. This helps to set a tone of positive expectations, countering the complaining that often mars family discussions. In addition, each family member is encouraged to compliment or give thanks to another family member. This is important because it provides an atmosphere of support within which discussion can take place openly, and differences of opinion will have a greater chance of being addressed as problems to be worked out rather than challenges to the relationship. If you sincerely compliment me or thank me for something specific I have done, I am more willing to listen to you and consider your point of view.

• The first agenda item is read and the family member who placed it on the agenda is asked if this is still a concern. (Or, if no formal agenda has been posted, each family member takes turns bringing up matters for discussion.) If the item is no longer a concern, the next agenda item is chosen. (Interestingly, many items placed on the agenda during the week turn out not to be a problem any more come family meeting day. The very act of writing the problem down often serves as a release of anger, which might be all that is needed. Also, some time has passed, and time, though not healing all wounds, does heal many of them.)

• If the agenda item is still a problem, the family member who raised the issue is asked what solution she thinks might best address it, after which all other family members are allowed to offer their solutions. Brainstorming is a particularly effective way to get ideas on the table at this point. A solution is chosen, preferably by consensus rather than majority rule (which tends to polarize), and the next item is addressed. When all issues have been addressed, the family might celebrate with a special dessert, story time, or game.

Why the structure and formality? In another time, in another place, we probably had no need for formal, structured family meetings. But today, when family members seem to be racing off in all different directions, rarely sitting down together to talk, with TV in many families creating a barrier to focused dialogue, with stresses and pressures unknown a generation ago (and with two out of three marriages taking place in 1990 predicted to end in divorce), we may very well need to intervene in a formal, structured way to compensate for the culture in which we live, and ensure that at least once a week all family members will be listened to and affirmed. The structure noted above need not be followed strictly; what is important is that we take the time to ensure that some format exists for family sharing, lest we live out our lives not ever really knowing what is on each other's minds.

One family I have met through my involvement in parenting classes uses a powerful teaching aid, called the Talking Stick, at their family meetings. The Talking Stick originates from Native American tribes in the Great Plains region. It is simply a stick, maybe a foot and a half to two feet long, decorated as desired with feathers, strips of leather, and beads, and held by the family meeting participant whose turn it is to talk. As long as the family member has the stick, she can talk without being interrupted.

But the Talking Stick does more than allow the holder to speak. It has a far more important function, for while the holder of the stick is talking, the other family members must be listening. In fact, the next person who wishes to speak may not do so until he has repeated back to the first speaker what she said, to her satisfaction. Only when the first person is satisfied that she has been listened to will the second person be allowed to speak.

So the Talking Stick is also a Listening Stick, in that through its presence all participants in the meeting are encouraged to listen carefully to the speaker, rather than planning ahead what they want to say. The Talking Stick serves, then, as a physical reminder of the importance of listening as the key to respectful communication.

What a public service it would be to send each member of Congress a Talking Stick!

There are a number of concerns that need to be addressed about family meetings if they are to effectively and respectfully involve all family members:

• A participant in one of our parenting classes during a discussion about family meetings once observed:

"We had family meetings when I was a kid. We all sat together around the dinner table with Dad at the head telling us what we were going to do, how we were going to do it, and when we were going to do it."

Clearly, that's not what we have in mind here. The purpose of the family meeting is to provide a process through which each family member can be listened to, have their ideas thoughtfully considered, and be affirmed. It is not a format for parental directing.

• Neither is the family meeting an opportunity for kid-bashing. There is a place for adult correction of children's behavior, but it should be done in private, in respect for the feelings of the child, not in the group setting of the family meeting. The family meeting should be a positive experience for all family members.

• The family meeting is not an abdication of parental responsibility. Providing a forum through which children can be listened to, considered, and affirmed does not mean that every idea they have is open to a family vote. The responsible family is the family that has aligned itself with basic principles, such as respectfulness, honesty, courtesy, and truthfulness. Further, the responsible family has made rules of conduct regarding curfews, television viewing, homework, household chores, etc. The family meeting may well provide a forum for the *discussion* of these items, but as responsibility ultimately lies with the parents, the decision must lie there as well. The effective family meeting is one in which all family members know what is open for debate and what is not, and the effective parent will ensure that the items not open for debate are limited to those that represent the basic family values and the rules that support them.

School-Smart Parenting Tip

Use family dinners, family meetings, and family nights to provide a safe haven in which your children can experience support, affirmation, communication, and a sense of belonging to something larger than themselves.

And when school problems confront them- work a bit too difficult, a teacher than seems unconcerned, classmates that are cruel-, they will be strengthened by the knowledge that there is a place called home in which they can find the peace and nurturance that will give them the support needed to make the best of each day.

Closing Time

No matter how hectic the day might be, and no matter how many negative experiences may have occurred, ending that day on a peaceful and positive note can go a long way toward providing the emotional stability that we are all striving for. We can not guarantee that our children's days will be filled with positive experiences, nor should we even try, but we can make a concerted effort to end the day in a reassuring and supportive manner. If our children can go to bed at peace about the day they have just completed, then they will be much better prepared to be positive about the day that is to come. Send them to bed angry and alienated, and they will find anger and alienation instead.

For that reason, many families have a designated "closing time," after which no more individual work is done and all family members can enjoy each other's company before it's time to turn out the lights and go to bed. Even if this is only for fifteen minutes, and even if Mom and Dad still have more to do before the evening is over, setting aside this time for the children to be together with the parents can be a very pleasant way to end their day.

At closing time, all homework, housework, and office work stops. The family comes together to close out the day with personal reflections, a story, a prayer, whatever best meets the family needs. Closing time helps to refocus the family on itself, to remind all family members that whatever has happened in each one's day, whatever directions each family member has taken, we now come together as a family to share some time together. What a pleasant way to end the day, one certain to provide a more peaceful sleep.

Television

I had a dream the other night. I dreamed that I was watching television and the opening scene of *Leave It to Beaver* was just coming on the screen. And there was The Beave, in black and white, walking home from school (*walking* home from school!), whistling in a happy and carefree manner, clicking a picket fence with a stick as he ambled along. If there were any troubles going on in the world, they were definitely not affecting The Beave.

I turned the dial (*turned the dial!*) and there appeared Andy Griffith as the sheriff and little Ron Howard as Opie strolling down a country lane together, fishing poles slung over their shoulders, with that so recognizable tune whistling in the background. If there were any problems in Mayberry, they were surely being put on hold for a day's fishing.

I turned the dial once again and there was Mary Tyler Moore, flipping her hat in the air, whistling the happiest of tunes- why did everybody whistle so much back then?- and, like Sheriff Andy, Opie, and The Beave, clearly without a care in the world.

And then I awoke. Hoping to prolong those pleasant memories and pursuing the fantasy that they just might linger if I wished for it hard enough, I rushed to the family room, picked up the remote, and started clicking away. With the first click, a very expensive sports car came on the screen, screeching through dark, wet, urban streets. In just a second or two, it crashed against a wall and burst into flames, bodies constrained and helpless inside. A second car came to an abrupt stop and the driver pulled out a semi-automatic and pumped a clipful of bullets into the writhing bodies inside, just in case.

I clicked the remote just in time to catch a well-known family sitcom just as the wife was badgering the husband for his lack of sexual prowess, and he in turn was attacking her for no longer having whatever it was that in earlier years had aroused that sexual prowess. I clicked once again and there was a talk show on and the audience, at the host's baiting, was screaming insults at a group of teenagers who were on the show because, they had complained, their parents never listen to them. The teenagers just sat there, shaking their heads, as if to say: "See what we mean!" I clicked once more and there was a victim of spousal abuse, her face still swollen from the latest attack, arguing in a panel discussion for stronger legislation against abusers. One more click and an advertisement for a top-selling beer tried to convince me that I would have a muscled, tanned, and youthful body if I would just use their product. I decided to go back to bed.

Is there a single invention of the past fifty years that has had more influence on our children than television? In 1954, the average American household spent about three hours a day watching TV; in 1994, it was up to seven. And there are no signs this is decreasing. Nor are there any signs that we will be returning soon to the days of *Mayberry RFD*, where our only childhood restraint was getting home before dark.

The computer has revolutionized the world of education, as well as the world of business, but its effect on young children, particularly those in the early years of schooling, is still minimal compared to television. This may change in time with the rapidly improving capabilities of the computer, including the increasing availability and potential of the Internet and similar services, but if it does it will only result in a replacement with even greater influence-

and no greater comfort for parents- than TV ever had. In fact, the computer may not only replace the TV as the dominant technology in the home, it may very well totally supplant it, making TV, as a separate and distinct unit in the house, obsolete. When home videos start coming to us through the computer, will it be long before the TV and the computer become one unit, a megacomputer/TV/video store all in one? The prospects are at once awesome and frightening.

But for now, television remains the dominant technological distraction for young children, and their most important teacher, a fact of particular note to parents of preschoolers, for whom the impact of television is at its greatest. Television is as familiar to our children as the furniture in their home; in fact, in many homes the television *is* the dominant piece of furniture.

Was there really life before television? What did people *do* back then? How did they entertain themselves? Believe it or not, there really was life before television and, risking oversimplification, it would be helpful to take a look at that life. Before TV came to dominate the family room, family members communicated. They discussed, played, gossiped . . . and, yes, argued, bickered, and fought. But there was communication. Adults communicated. Children communicated. And interpersonal skills were developed. Television drastically altered all that, resulting in family members interacting not with each other but with a box that grew to assume a status larger than any one of us, indeed, larger than all of us put together. Television disrupted the most important language lesson in a child's life, family conversation.

And not content with the altering of family patterns that took place in the family room, we invited the television into the dining area.

The one remaining setting in our homes where we are almost forced to communicate, sitting next to and opposite each other around a table, soon shared the fate of the family room. All eyes focus now on the increasingly dominating box, instead of on those who share our real world as we break bread each evening. And in many American homes, the dining area is not even used on a regular basis, as each family member grabs a dinner and heads for the TV. And we ask ourselves why kids can't communicate any more. (And to further complicate the problem, a 1994 Gallup poll reported that fifty-eight percent of American children now have TV sets in their *bedrooms.*)

Add to all this the content of television as it has evolved over the years, and the problem compounds. We've come a long way since *Leave it to Beaver.* We laugh today at Ward Cleaver reading the paper in the evening, still dressed in his jacket and tie, and June Cleaver vacuuming the carpet in her pumps and pearls, but what did we learn about family values and interpersonal relationships from *Leave it to Beaver* . . . (or, for a later generation, from *Little House on the Prairie,* and, still later, *The Cosby Show*) and what do we learn today from *The Simpsons, Roseanne,* and *Married . . . with Children?*

I know what *I* learned from *Leave it to Beaver.* As silly as the show was, as contrived as some of the problems may have been, as little as my family had in common with the Cleavers, I identified with them. I grew up in a home that was distinctly unlike the Cleavers, in a large city that had few of the suburban Norman Rockwellesqe images of the Cleavers' town, and in a family that included four times as many children, that was still very close to its immigrant roots, that was non-Anglo-Saxon, and non-affluent. And yet in spite of all this, my dad was Ward, my mom- who I can't ever remember *seeing* in pumps and pearls, much less vacuuming the carpet in them- was June, I was Wally, and one of my several younger brothers was The Beave.

And what did I learn watching that show? I learned how siblings were supposed to talk to one another. I learned how spouses were supposed to talk to one another. I learned about the respect that children showed their parents . . . and the respect that parents showed their children.

I learned there were good guys and there were not-so-good guys- remember Eddie Haskell? And I learned that the not-so-good guys were not to be hated, but to be supported. I learned that there were unpopular kids in the world- remember Lumpy?- but that I was called upon not to criticize them but, again, to support them. I learned, in short, positive life lessons, which I am happy to be able to say were also taught, more often than not, in school, in church, and in my home. I grew up seeing TV as an extension and reflection of my value system, as a reinforcement of what I learned in school, church, and home. But who today can say the same?

Zig Ziglar, the motivational speaker and writer who has popularized the power of positive thinking for several generations of Americans, has a trademark saying that is very appropriate here: "You are what you are because of what you put into your head; if you want to change what you are, you need to change what you put into your head." We might well ask what is being put into our children's heads. It's not a pleasant thought.

How do we compensate for all this, short of throwing out the TV. Although there are families who have taken this step (and should probably be applauded for it), most of us are not prepared to do so.

How then do we compensate for the threat to the development of interpersonal skills and values of our children?

Step One is recognizing the problem, that TV does in fact present major challenges for us as we strive to provide emotional stability in the home. Step Two is understanding it- what are the problems TV presents, why are they problems for us, and what steps might be available to us to overcome or compensate for those problems? And Step Three is making the decision to take the identified steps, be they formal family meetings, restricted TV time, scheduled one-on-one attention, and/or TV-free dinner. The important thing is to address the problem and gain control of the television so that it does not gain control of us. Quite a challenge, but one worth taking.

Physical Signs of Affection

At the close of a long day some years back during which I had successfully ignored my family, living instead almost entirely within my emotional cave, my son, about twelve at the time, approached me, and with the simplicity that is found only in youth said, "Dad, you haven't hardly even touched me all day!" And he was right. My silence he could handle. My characteristic introspection was something he had learned was just part of the way old Dad is. But the fact that not once during the day had I hugged him, patted his shoulder, or even punched him playfully in the arm was more than he could handle. "You haven't hardly even touched me all day." What a powerful indictment!

Communication, the experts tell us, is only about twenty percent verbal. The remaining eighty percent is body language, intonation, context, setting, attitude, etc. The raised eye brow, the folded arms, the blank stare, the tone of voice, and physical position in relation to the listener all affect the message that is received. And nothing is more important than physical touch.

It is unfortunate today that physical touch has become such a sensitive issue because of abuse problems. Teachers are routinely instructed by administrators to avoid touching a student lest that touch be misconstrued, resulting in embarrassment, discomfort, confrontation, law suits, or worse. And some parents have even taken this approach to the problem and applied it to their own families, avoiding physical signs of affection lest their children grow up unwary of its abuses.

Concern about this is, of course, justified- we do not need to be reminded that abuses do occur and must be guarded against. But when our vigilance in preventing abuse leads us to argue for no physical touch at all, we are contributing to another form of abuse, the abuse of emotional detachment. We have all read reports of the critical need for physical touch in new-borns, how picking a child up, holding him close, stroking his face can be critical to his very survival. People who work in nursing homes tell us that physical touch can make a difference in the quality of life of the elderly, even prolonging their lives. Men and women throughout the world regularly shake hands, embrace, or kiss each other in their daily greeting. We all need physical touch, and we need it regularly.

Emotional stability in the home is strengthened when family members regularly touch each other affectionately. In addition to making contact, providing closeness, and showing affection, loving physical touch helps children understand the difference between touch that is appropriate and that which isn't. Spouses can model appropriate physical touch by their own natural expressions of it to each other, as well as to their children. Our children will have plenty of opportunities from television and the movies to learn how hugs and kisses can be abused; they need to learn from us that they are natural signs of affection that happy, healthy, emotionally secure people can express without fear.

One final note on the issue of physical touch: I do not believe that there is any room for corporal punishment in the family that is striving for emotional stability. I can think of nothing that corporal punishment teaches other than power, force, violence, and pain. I see no logical connection between spanking and teaching; indeed, I see it as an abdication of our parental responsibility to teach through example. It is truly unfortunate that, as reported by a Gallup poll in December 1995, about half of American parents believe it is "sometimes necessary to discipline a child with a good, hard spanking." This is a very sad commentary on the state of parenting and parent education, and it presents a challenge for all of us who would strive for a more respectful way of guiding our children. Let's ensure that the physical contact we have with our children is always loving, soothing, and comforting, and never the source of pain.

School-Smart Parenting Tip

Avoid all forms of negative physical contact,
including spanking.

Let's not teach our children that imposing physical pain on others is an acceptable way to get them to do what we want them to do, lest they transfer those negative lessons
to school in the form of physical aggression.

Consequences, Not Punishments

When our daughter, Jennifer, was in her second year of high school, we found ourselves caught up in a rescuing situation that we had not anticipated and that, consequently, had developed into a major problem. Jennifer attends a high school that is some twenty miles from our home. She rides a school bus, but the nearest stop for that bus is also distant from our home, some five miles away, close to where Carol works. Since the bus stop is nearer to Carol's place of work than to mine, it has fallen to her to drive Jennifer to the school bus each morning. As a result, Carol also found herself assuming the job of waking Jennifer up on time to drive with her to the bus stop. Since Jennifer had no other options for getting to school other than riding with Mom to the bus stop, Mom felt that it was her duty to go into her room- six, eight, ten times each morning- to rouse Jennifer from her bed and drag her, if necessary, to the car.

What were the consequences if Jennifer refused to get up and get dressed on time for Mom to take her to the bus stop? There were natural consequences- she wouldn't get to school that day- and there were logical consequences- for failing to accept the responsibility of getting to school each day during the week, she would lose the privilege of going out over the weekend. The consequences were discussed with and agreed to by Jennifer. They were in place and they were clear. But it wasn't working.

It wasn't working, so it initially appeared, because Mom's day- and, more often than not, Jennifer's day- was ruined by the battle that took place each morning to get Jennifer out of bed. And so in frustration, Mom let it all out one evening. "Why do I have to deal with this every morning? How come you don't have to battle with your daughter (*your* daughter!) and ruin every day. And how come all this business about natural and logical consequences isn't working, Mr. Parenting Expert!"

With all the sensitivity a man typically shows to a woman's emotional display of frustration, I jumped immediately into a problem-solving mode (which was exactly what Carol did *not* want right then) and embarked upon an explanation of the distinction between natural and logical consequences, why they are effective in most situations, and why Carol was not allowing them to be effective in this situation and was thereby creating all her own problems.

About a week later, after all the dust had settled, we were able to calmly and intelligently discuss Jennifer's morning problems. What we came to realize, after much discussion and debate, was that in fact we were not allowing the consequences to take place. By going into the room six, eight, ten times to ensure that Jennifer was getting up, we were stepping in and preventing her from experiencing the consequences of her actions. We were, in short, rescuing her.

Why were we doing this? Why would we step in every day and rescue Jennifer from experiencing what would happen if she failed to take responsibility for getting herself up, something a fifteen-year-old could certainly do by herself? Why were we preventing her from growing in maturity through the experience of real-life lessons? Why? Because it hurt us too much to see her miss school and, possibly, miss a big dance, party, or evening with friends over the weekend.

The dialogue that took place next between Mom and Dad was quite revealing. Why do you go in there so often every morning?, I asked. Because she won't get up on her own. But why can't we just let her experience the consequences of missing school and weekend activities? Because this weekend is her school's homecoming dance, and next weekend is her friend's sixteenth birthday party, and the weekend after that they are all going to Six Flags together, and the weekend after that . . . Well, then, I responded, with characteristic sensitivity, unless you plan to spend the rest of your life waking up Jennifer in the morning, you'd better learn to accept the unpleasantness of a missed weekend.

So we sat down with Jennifer and frankly and honestly explained the problem from our perspective. We talked about the consequences that were already in place, checked out with her whether or not she was still comfortable with those consequences (she was), went out and purchased a back-up battery-operated alarm to go with her electric radio alarm, told her that starting with the coming week we would go into her room just twice to help her get up (this is called weaning: rather than go "cold turkey" with her, we limited our involvement to twice each morning, then a few months later to once, and finally to not at all), reminded her what was going on next weekend (it was the weekend of her friend's sixteenth birthday party), shook hands and called it a deal.

Monday came and Jennifer was awake and eating breakfast even before we had awakened. On Tuesday, she was still asleep when we awoke, and when her alarms went off she remained in bed. But on the second visit from Mom she was up and ready. Then came Wednesday, which turned out to be The Day of Reckoning.

Mom and I got up at our regular times. Jennifer's radio alarm went off as it always did, followed five minutes later by her battery-operated alarm. Both the radio was playing (too loud, of course) and the alarm was buzzing, but Jennifer remained under the covers. Mom went in the first time, shook her gently, got the usual muffled response, and left. Ten minutes later, she repeated the procedure, getting the same response. On Tuesday, that had resulted in Jennifer's joining us at the breakfast table. But today, no one was emerging from her room.

The minutes ticked away with only a half hour remaining before Mom would have to leave, and still no Jennifer. Maybe I ought to check inside just one more time, she wondered. My body language said no.

Twenty minutes before Mom would have to leave, and still no Jennifer. But maybe I didn't shake her hard enough the second time, Mom suggested. Let her be, was my reply.

Ten minutes before leaving time, and no Jennifer. Mom protested: But Saturday is the big sixteenth birthday party. I can't just let her miss it! I answered: Nobody wants her to miss that party, but we need to let the consequences take place. Let her be. (It's so easy to be firm when the *other* parent will end up receiving the brunt of the child's wrath!) And so we both left for work, leaving Jennifer behind, allowing her to wake up some time later to realize what had happened and deal with it on her own throughout the day.

When we got home that evening, we resisted the temptation to dump on Jennifer- Look what happened! How can you be so irresponsible! How many times did we tell you to get up as soon as your alarm goes off! When will you ever grow up?!?- and instead allowed her to share her own disappointment with us. When she asked, as was inevitable, whether this really meant that she had to miss the party, we simply reminded her what the arrangement was that we had all agreed to, and we left it at that. She asked us two or three more times the next few days, and we gave the same answer. But there were no tantrums about the missed party.

When Saturday night came and there were no plans of our own to go anywhere, we rented a video and the three of us- Mom, Dad, and Jennifer- stayed home and enjoyed each other's company. Did Jennifer miss the party? Very much so. Did it hurt- both her and us? Again, very much so. But it's been a full year now, and she has never failed to get up on time for school since. We are confident that she learned from the experience, and years from now, when she is out there in the "real world," we are confident that her employers will always be able to count on her to get to work every day and on time.

What made it all work was the use of consequences rather than punishment. Jennifer was not punished for failing to get up on time for school; instead, she was allowed to experience the consequences of her actions. What's the difference? The difference lies in how we approach the situation, and how, as a result of our approach, the child perceives what happens to her. As a consequential approach to working with children is a key ingredient in teaching for responsibility- along with unconditional love, specific feedback, clear limits established in advance, and firmness with dignity and respect-, it's worth our time to take a closer look at this.

Natural consequences are those that eventuate naturally, with no interference on the part of the parent. If a child goes outside on a cold day without a sweater on, she will get cold. If she goes outside when it's raining without an umbrella, she will get wet. If she fails to get up on time for school, she will be late or miss school entirely. If she plays in heavy traffic, she will most likely get hurt.

Clearly, some natural consequences we can allow to happen and others we cannot. When the consequences are too long-range for our children to understand (not brushing your teeth, for example) or too dangerous for them (playing in traffic), natural consequences are not appropriate. And some natural consequences may be dependent upon the maturity level of our children, or upon our own personal or family values. It may or may not be a good idea to let her go outside on a cold day without a sweater on. It may or may not be a good idea to allow her to experience the natural consequences of a dirty room or missing a day of school. These are choices we must make based on our own wisdom and experiences.

But the important thing about natural consequences is that we adults need not do anything to assist them; they simply eventuate, with no effort on our part. And if we choose in a given situation to rely on natural consequences, our best approach to them is to just let them happen . . . and keep our mouths shut afterwards, avoiding the adultisms that can turn a natural consequence into a punishment in the child's eyes.

When natural consequences are not appropriate or effective, we can use logical consequences. Logical consequences are those consequences that need to be devised by the parents, preferably in dialogue with the child, and applied to specific situations. To be most effective, they should be *related* to the problem, *reasonable* in consideration of the problem, and handled *respectfully,* thereby avoiding the creation of a bigger problem . . . and they need to be *perceived by the child* as related, reasonable, and respectful. These Three R's of Logical Consequences- related, reasonable, and respectful- help us ensure that we don't fall into the trap of using consequences as just a nicer way to punish.

Consequences are qualitatively distinct from punishments.

Punishments are what *we do to children,* consequences are what happen naturally or logically *as a result of the choices they make.* Consequences are not just a nicer way to impose our demands; they are outcomes we experience and learn from. (And by the way, if you find yourself saying "*suffer* the consequences" instead of "*experience* the consequences," you are probably dealing with punishment, not consequences.)

In working with Jennifer regarding her getting up on time for school, we had both natural and logical consequences working. The natural consequences of not getting up on time were simply that she missed school and would most likely fall behind in her work. An argument could be made that that's enough of a consequence and that there should be no need for establishing logical consequences in this situation. But school was a much lower priority for Jennifer at that time than it was for us, and we feared, with good reason, that she would be willing to miss a day every now and then if the only consequence was falling behind in her work.

So we sat down with Jennifer and decided upon logical consequences, agreeing that the privilege of going out with friends over the weekend would be dependent upon her accepting and fulfilling the responsibility of going to school. Is this related? We think so- note the connection between privileges and responsibilities. Is it reasonable? Again, we think so: If she misses school during the week, she loses the privilege of going out for just that weekend, not for the whole month. (It is the *inevitability* of the consequence, not its *severity,* that matters most here; in fact, severity is frequently counterproductive as it tends to lead to rebellion.) Was it handled respectfully, both beforehand and after? We did our best to ensure that it was.

Again, the opposite of a consequential approach is punishment. And the difference is not in what happens, so much as it is in how the whole experience is perceived by the child. We could have simply punished Jennifer for not getting up on time. We could have had no discussion about the problem. We could have simply declared that she was grounded for the weekend . . . or for the month . . . or "forever." We could have worked hard to make sure that during her grounding she "suffered," rather than have the opportunity for a fun evening watching a video with her parents. We could have dumped adultism upon adultism on top of her. We could have shamed, blamed, and criticized her for not being responsible.

But if we had done so, what would her perception of the experience have been? What would she have learned from the experience? Would she have learned that when she makes certain choices in life, those choices carry with them, of necessity, certain specific consequences? Or would she have learned that life consists of other people doing things to you?

Therein lies the difference between a consequential approach and a punishment approach to working with children. In the former, my choices determine what happens to me; in the latter, what happens is what other people do to me. Striving for a home environment in which consequences are the rule and punishments are the exception will help provide the emotional stability that results from the perception that the outcomes that I experience result from the choices that I make. And there is no better road to responsibility than that.

Consequences, Not Rewards

Interestingly, all that has been said above regarding consequences vs. punishments applies just as well to consequences vs. rewards, although the hazards of a rewards-based environment may not be as obvious as those of a punishment-based environment. For a fascinating look at the dangers implicit in rewards-based systems, see Alfie Kohn's provocative study, *Punished By Rewards*. For now, suffice it to say that rewards can serve as little better than another way to control others ("Do what I want you to do and I will give you this."), that they tend to be disruptive of relationships because they focus on winners and losers, that they ignore the root causes of problems, and that they discourage risk-taking and creativity. Indeed, a good argument could be made that rewards are even worse than punishments, because rewards take a positive thing and ruin it, whereas punishment only takes a negative thing and makes it worse.

To the degree to which we can take advantage of natural and logical consequences rather than rewards when working with our children, they will learn to appreciate their achievements as valued in and of themselves, rather than because of a reward they get. If we give our child $5 for getting an 'A' on her report card, we are communicating to her that the reason for getting the 'A' is the $5. If, instead, we sit down with her and ask her why she thinks she was able to get such a good grade, what she learned from the experiences that led up to the 'A,' and how she can use that information to transfer her success in that area to other areas of her life, we will be helping her take that experience and maximize its value. And we will be demonstrating our real interest in her achievements, something that is worth well in excess of $5.

School-Smart Parenting Tip

Think consequences, rather than rewards and punishments.
Teach that what happens to us is largely a result of what
we do, rather than what other people do to us.

In school, our children will be more inclined to see that the
choices they make result in the outcomes they experience,
leading to improved effort, motivation, and achievement.

Leaving School Issues at School and Home Issues at Home

Now for the last word on rewards, punishments, and consequences: Let the teachers deal with school issues and the parents with home issues. If our children get in trouble at school and receive some consequence for that- time out, missed recess, detention-, there is no need for us to complicate the matter by adding to that consequence at home. I have seen too many examples of home/school communication breaking down because children fail to tell their parents about school problems out of fear that they will be punished at home.

When we are apprised of school problems, all that we need to do is verbally demonstrate our support for the school's concern and interest and sit down with our child and ask him what happened, why it happened, and what he can do next time to avoid the problem. That's all. The school doesn't need to apply discipline for at-home infractions, and we parents do not need to apply discipline for at-school infractions. All that is needed is mutual support and the willingness to work with the child to help him see what he can do to avoid the problem the next time.

If we handle school discipline problems that way we increase the possibility that our children will communicate with us about them. Otherwise, they will work diligently to keep those problems from us, even to the extent of destroying teacher notes, changing report card grades, and lying. Support and encouragement yield open communication; criticism and punishment yield avoidance and rebellion. The choice is clear.

School-Smart Parenting Tip

Leave school problems at school and home problems at home. If your child gets in trouble at school, work with her to identify what happened, why it happened, and what can be done next time to avoid it. But don't add your own discipline to school discipline.

Our children will appreciate the confidence that we have in their ability to work through their school problems without our over-involvement, and they will be more willing to keep us informed of those problems.

"Because I said so!"

How many times have you found yourself using expressions with your children that your parents used on you? And you swore you'd never use them on your own children. We all do it, not because we want to, but because we haven't taken the time to identify alternatives to those tired, old sayings. Rather than reflect on what we would really like to say, we just replay the old scripts that are deep within our memory bank. We want to be more affirming- at least more creative!- but we have never stopped to think about just how.

Well, let's stop to think about it now. Let's take a look at some of those dreaded expressions and come up with alternatives. And let's really shock our kids the next time we have an unpleasant encounter with them by using a new expression, a firm yet respectful expression, that will enable them to focus on the problem at hand, rather than get distracted by our sarcasms. The following examples are taken from a very informal survey of students ages six through fourteen that was conducted at a certain Dallas-area elementary school that I have some association with:

The Old Script	The New and Improved Script
"Because I said so."- suggests that the reason that you should do certain things rather than other things is simply my arbitrary decision.	"Because it's the right thing to do."- suggests that the reason that you should do certain things rather than other things is the intrinsic worthiness or

correctness of those things.

"No one ever said life is fair."- discounts the child's feelings and communicates the perception that life is just that way and there's nothing you can do about it.

"I can understand how you might feel that way. And I share your wish that life would be fair. Now how can we make the best of this situation?"- affirms the child's feelings and communicates that we can still influence outcomes even if life isn't fair.

"What part of 'NO' don't you understand?"- OK, maybe this was cute the first dozen or so times we said it, but it's old now and its only value is as sarcasm- which is no value at all. Sarcasm only teaches children to be sarcastic; it doesn't teach respectfulness.

"The reason I am saying 'no' is because this matter is very important to me. Later, when you are ready to discuss this respectfully, I will do my best to explain it to you."- communicates that there are some matters in life that the parent must assume responsibility for, whether or not the child likes it, but does so respectfully and communicates a willingness to explain the reason.

"If everyone jumped off the cliff, would you do likewise?"- besides having no relevance whatsoever to the issue at stake, this expression prevents us from accepting the opportunity of communicating our family values.

"I can understand your wanting to go, particularly if some of your friends are going. But as we discussed yesterday at our family meeting, we do not go to those movies because we believe they communicate values that we find very disrespectful."- this addresses the specific issue directly and respectfully and communicates the reason for the decision, while at the same time reaffirming the family's values.

"When I was your age . . . "- when used to tell a story in a friendly setting, this can be a very effective way to share our past with our children, and they will listen with anticipation; if it is used to show our children how tougher we are or how smarter we are or how much better they have it now (and why don't you appreciate that?), it only serves to miss the opportunity to share our past in a way that

"I can remember when I was young, we used to . . . "- since we have by and large lost the opportunity to use "when I was your age . . . " without causing a rolling of the eyes, it's probably best to try a different opener; the important point is that we should avoid trying to communicate our superiority ("When I was in school, we

allows them to enjoy the experience.

had to *memorize The Midnight Ride of Paul Revere,* not just know who wrote it!") when telling stories about our past if we want our children to listen to them, learn from them, and be willing to share more with us.

As you might imagine, the students had a lot of fun identifying their most hated expressions. There were more- a lot more!- but those noted above constitute the top five.

One very interesting comment by a younger student was quite enlightening- "Mom's voice changes when she talks about me in public- it's all squeaky and baby-like." Why do we do that? Why do we treat our developing young people as if their development were arrested at the infancy stage? Why don't we just talk to them and about them the same way we speak to and about adults? What communication skills- infantile or adult-like- do we want to model for our children?

Two themes were common to the expressions that the students identified- sarcasm and authoritarianism. Sarcastic expressions ("Are you waiting for a personal invitation?", "I hope you have a kid just like you!") led the list, followed closely by authoritarian ones ("Because I'm your mother.", "I'm the parent; you're the child."). Our challenge as parents is to avoid sarcasm and authoritarianism by modeling the prescription of positive discipline identified by Jane Nelsen- firmness, with dignity and respect.

"Firmness" communicates what needs to be done *authoritatively,*

214

which, contrary to the word 'authoritarian,' suggests a higher authority or reason or principle, to which we *all* are subject, Mom and Dad as well as the children. "With dignity and respect" reminds us that our children do not occupy some lower level of the species than we do, and they really do deserve to be treated respectfully, just as we ourselves deserve to be treated.

We can change the words we use if we make the conscious effort to identify the words that do damage, actively substitute more respectful words, and put them into practice. We will feel better about it, and our children will feel better about it. And they will reap the benefit of having learned positive and affirming expressions to use in their interactions with their own children when they become parents. Not a bad gift to give them!

Problem-Solving with Empathy

We most frequently get careless with the words we use with our children when we are criticizing them for something they have done wrong. And we do this because our knee jerk reaction is to focus on blame, rather than on finding a solution to the problem. Therefore, a good first step in improving our verbal response to problems with our children is to make the perceptual shift from focusing on blame to focusing on solutions. If I can change my approach when dealing with my child's homework problems, for example, from "How many times do I have to tell you to get your homework done before bedtime?" to "It appears that our previous plan about getting all your homework done before bedtime isn't working, so let's talk about another plan," then I have set the stage for an approach that involves the child as an agent in the solution to his problem.

Once having recognized the problem as needing a solution, rather than just needing blame, and having done so respectively, we are ready to work through the problem. There are any number of ways that a problem-solving process can be broken down into various components; the following six-step approach is one that I have found particularly helpful:

1. Ask the child why he thinks he is having difficulty with the problem. Listen carefully to what he has to say in an effort to understand his perceptions and get into his world. In checking his perceptions, avoid as much as possible the 'why' word, which tends to come across as interrogatory and accusatory, often resulting in an "I don't know." Use "What would be some reasons that you think you're having problems with this?" rather than "Why are you having problems with this?"

2. Reflect back to the child what your understanding is of what he has said, checking with him to make sure that you've got it right: "Let me be sure I understand what you're saying here. You're saying that you think you're having trouble getting your homework done before bedtime because you put off starting it until it's too late. You don't like starting it as soon as you get home and then you keep putting it off. And the more you put it off, the bigger the job seems to get. Is that right?"

3. Show empathy for the problem: "Well, I can understand that. I usually like a break too right after I get home from work before I jump into any chores at home. As a matter of fact, I can remember

back when I was in school and homework was the last thing I wanted to do as soon as I got home."

4. Check for ideas from your child. Often, if we have handled the discussion respectfully and have demonstrated real interest in our child's thoughts on the issue, he will be able to come up with solutions on his own at this point.

5. Share your own thoughts on the problem, but continue to involve the child in the solution: "What do you think would happen if you took a short break right after you got home and then did just one part of your homework? Then you could go out and play, maybe come in a bit early before dinner and work a little more, then finish it up after dinner. Sometimes when we break a large task into smaller parts and spread them out it's easier. Do you think that might work?" Notice that we've avoided lecturing here, offering our suggestion in the form of a question: "What do you think would happen if . . . "

6. Agree on a solution, either one that your child mentioned, one that you mentioned, or some combination of the two. Agree to check back in a week or two to see how the plan is working.

When we shift from blaming to problem solving we take the pressure off our children and allow them to take ownership of the problem. We offer our own wisdom and experience as a resource, but we keep the child focused on solving his problem. Criticizing, on the other hand, lets the child off the hook. The homework problem becomes Dad's, not the child's, whose only problem is waiting out the verbal barrage. Once the shaming and blaming is over, the child is home free, and Dad is left with his own frustration . . . and an unresolved problem that he will no doubt take responsibility for bringing up again tomorrow night. So the decision is clear: If you want to be responsible for the problem, shame, blame, and criticize your child; if you want *him* to be responsible, engage in problem-solving with empathy.

Keep Your Mouth Shut and Act

One of my favorite cartoons shows a man lecturing to his dog. What the man is saying is this: "How many times do I have to tell you, Rover, that you're not supposed to scratch the furniture. I just bought this furniture last week! It isn't even paid for yet, and now it has these scratches all over it! Do I have to leave you outside all day? Do I have to return you to the pound? What do I have to do to get you to behave?" And what the dog is hearing is this: "Blah, blah, blah, blah, Rover, blah, blah, blah, blah, blah . . ."

I think of that cartoon whenever I find myself lecturing to my children. And I know that the more I lecture, the more I sound like the man in the cartoon. And the more my children hear what Rover hears: "Blah, blah, blah, blah, blah, blah, blah . : ."

In working with our children, less is often best. The more we say, the more they tune us out. And the fewer words we use, the more they hear what we are saying. State your concerns, firmly, respectfully, and in brief; then, keep your mouth shut and act.

Take Care of Your Own Needs

Whenever I fly, I find myself intrigued by the words of the flight attendant as he explains how to use the oxygen masks: "If you are flying with a small child, apply your own oxygen mask to yourself first, then help your child apply his." The implication is clear: You will be of no help to your child if you do not first ensure that you are taken care of. Once you are safe, you can give your full attention to the needs of your child.

This is a perfect metaphor for the importance of us parents ensuring that our own needs are met in order that we might effectively provide for our own emotional stability as well as that of our children. If I am drained of energy, if I have had no time all day to be alone with myself, if I feel unloved, I need to attend to those

219

needs first or I will be ineffective in meeting my children's needs.

What gets in the way of this is guilt. Guilt is that little voice within us that tells us that what we are doing is not quite right. As such, guilt has much value, and we have all encountered people in our lives who could use a little bit more of it.

But guilt is often overused. We feel guilt when we are not rushing to school to bail our children out of the little problems they have gotten themselves into. We feel guilt if we are not attending to their every needs. We feel guilt if we are not entertaining them, reading to them, playing with them . . . all the time. We feel guilt . . . until we are totally drained of energy and love, robbing us of our ability to deal with our children effectively and leaving us with nothing to fall back on but the knee jerk reactions that we have been working so hard to overcome- blaming, shaming, directing, criticizing, scolding, yelling.

To avoid this, we need to accept the fact of our own needs . . . without guilt. We need to do something for ourselves- go off alone with a good book, call a friend to go out for lunch, take a warm bath, go shopping. We need to announce this, without apology, to our family. And then we will experience the renewal that allows us to be at our best- for ourselves, our children, and our spouse.

A Place Where You Want to Be

What all this adds up to- family dinners, family meetings, and family nights; physical signs of affection; alternatives to TV; logical consequences rather than punishment; respectful rather than critical language; problem solving rather than blaming; self-renewal- is a home environment in which the child feels welcome and comfortable. Is the home a place where our children want to be? When choices arise between staying home with the family and engaging in unhealthy activities, will they choose, instead, to stay home? Will they be comfortable inviting their friends over? Starting early to make sure that the home is a comfortable place to be- a place of encouragement, support, and affirmation; a place where each person is loved unconditionally; a place free from constant nagging and criticism- will increase the probability that we will be able to answer those questions affirmatively, thereby providing the oasis that our children need and deserve.

All You Need Is Love

The home characterized by emotional stability is the home in which love is given freely, not in response to anything the child (or spouse) does or does not do. When we tell our children that we love them for the grades they are receiving or for the work they did around the house or for the gift they have just given us, we communicate that love is something given in return for something else. But true love is given freely, unconditionally, and because of who you are, not because of what you do. Three vignettes flesh this out nicely for me, and I hope they do the same for you.

The first is from the television series *Little House on the Prairie,* every episode of which I believe I have seen at least twice, the consequence of having a young daughter in the family during the life of the series. Watching *Little House on the Prairie* was something Jennifer insisted that I do with her, and, frankly, I enjoyed the experience . . . and the show. (Of course, Michael Landon was an old hero of mine from the *Bonanza* days.)

If you remember *Little House on the Prairie,* then you remember Harriet Olsen and her long-suffering husband, Nels. Harriet was- how can we put this delicately?- *difficult.* In fact, if she had a single redeeming feature, she hid it from us well. She was mean-spirited, vindictive, and, to top it all off, made up to appear downright ugly.

But in this one episode, Harriet showed the vaguest indication of latent goodness. You had to look very carefully, but it was there. I can't remember the details that led up to the episode, but I do remember the scene. Harriet, who had done something so horrible that even she was embarrassed by it, was sitting in her dining room, bemoaning her own nastiness, sniveling about what a terrible person she was, and crying out for some sign of redemption, when Nels, sitting next to her and holding her hand, looked into her eyes and said, simply, "Harriet, I love you. *I* love you." Harriet's face shone with a radiance that was brief but revealing, and I have not seen that radiance on any other episode.

The second vignette is from my favorite motion picture of all time, *The Wizard of Oz.* In this particular scene, Dorothy, the Scarecrow, the Cowardly Lion, and the Tin Woodsman have just returned to Oz with the captured broomstick of the Wicked Witch of the West. When they ask for the Wizard's promises to them to be fulfilled, he tries to put them off. But Dorothy and her pals will have none of it- they did what they were challenged to do, and now it was the Wizard's turn to fulfill his promises to them. Confronted with no alternative after Toto reveals his secret, the Wizard rises to the occasion and addresses their concerns. He shows the Scarecrow that he always had a brain, and he just needed some recognition in the form of a diploma. He shows the Cowardly Lion that he always had courage, and he just needed recognition in the form of a medal.

And he shows the Tin Woodsman that his heart was always beating—he just needed to be recognized in the form of a testimonial. And then, placing his hand on the Woodsman's tin shoulder, the Wizard says: "And remember, my sentimental friend, the heart is not judged by how much *you* love, but by how much you are loved by others."

And the third and final vignette is the story of a little girl, Jessica, who lives with her grandmother. It is Grandma's birthday, and little Jessica has nothing to give her, but on the way home from school she spots some dandelions in a field and picks a bunch. She sneaks them into the house when her grandmother isn't looking, finds an old vase, fills it with water, arranges the dandelions as best she can, and, beaming, presents them: "Grandma, I picked these flowers for you. Happy birthday!"

Grandma, not anticipating the gift and so seeing a vase filled with weeds rather than Jessica's present, exclaims: "Well, thank you, Jessica, but these aren't flowers, these are weeds." And little Jessica replies: "If you love them, Grandma, they are no longer weeds."

And sometimes it all comes down to that simple truth: If you love them, they are no longer weeds. Harriet Olsen is able to show the goodness that is deep within her only when Nels expresses his love for her. The Tin Woodsman is reminded that the love of others is the guarantee of the love that is very much within him. And little Jessica knows, in the simple wisdom of a child, that if love can move mountains it can certainly turn weeds into flowers.

The home characterized by emotional stability is the home where love can turn weeds into flowers. In such a home, all family members experience the security of knowing that whatever they may face in the outside world, when they walk through the doors of their home they will be accepted, affirmed, loved. Children raised in such a home are children who can go freely and confidently into that outside world, including school, knowing that they are loved and lovable, fully open to all that that world can offer. They enter the world of schooling with their potentials fully maximized. They go into it without any unnecessary baggage weighing them down, which would prevent them from fully participating in the opportunities provided by school. And they go into that world knowing that when adversity hits, and it will, they have that warm, safe place called home to return to. And this is the greatest gift we can give them.

CHAPTER 7

WALKING THE TALK:
ROLE MODELING

Example is not the main thing in influencing others.
It is the only thing.

-Albert Schweitzer

Given these three behaviors- providing opportunities for contribution by organizing the family for household chores, affirming our children by showing real interest in their interests, and providing emotional stability in the home- how do we parents organize our *own* lives to maximize the possibility of our children learning from these behaviors and experiencing success and happiness during their school years? The key to this question lies in the recognition that we cannot change other people, not even our own children. (Not even our spouses: How many marriages do you know that have fallen on rocky ground in spite of one spouse's anticipation that the other would change . . . after marriage?) We can only change ourselves; but in doing so, we can offer a model of positive change for others to emulate.

When basketball superstar Charles Barkley of the Houston Rockets and the Olympics "Dream Team" responded to critics of his life style that he did not consider it his responsibility to be a role model, that his responsibility was to be a professional basketball player and win games, and that it was the *parents'* responsibility to be their children's role models, he was right and he was wrong. He was wrong because it truly is the responsibility of every man and woman on earth to be a role model, and the more visible we are in the public eye, the greater that responsibility is. And for sports figures, who occupy a place of near reverence for young people, the responsibility to be a role model grows in proportion to their fame.

But he was right when he correctly identified the responsibility of the parent in "walking the talk" if we want our children to listen to our words. In other words, the old adultism "do what I say, not what I do" doesn't work. Or rather, it does work, if what we want are children who grow up telling *their* children to "do what I say, not what I do." Highlight it, underline it, write it on a file card and tape it to your mirror: There is no more effective way to teach than through "walking the talk," what we more familiarly refer to as role modeling.

We've all heard the three most important things to know about real estate: location, location, location. Without too much exaggeration, it could be said that the three most important things to know about parenting are: role modeling, role modeling, role modeling. Role modeling is nothing more than the decision to look at what *I* need to do, rather than to what *my children* need to do, and then following through.

What follows are twelve specific ways that we parents can role
model effective behaviors for our children during their school years.
Some of these are reaffirmations of points made in previous
chapters, with the emphasis now placed on our own active modeling
of the behaviors. Others are new challenges for our reflection and
consideration. In all cases, the emphasis is placed on the importance
of "walking the talk" so that our children will witness the integration
of actions and values that makes them more willing to learn from us.

1. Respect time commitments.

Have you ever been frustrated by the spouse, friend, or employee
who is seldom on time? Have you found their excuses- "Oh, I'm
just late for everything; that's just the way I am!"- somewhat less
than satisfying? Are you struggling yourself with a negative
mindsct that is justifying continual tardiness in yourself or in your
children? If so, it's helpful to realize that being on time is nothing
more than a habit, and habits can be changed. And if we wish to

change the habit of tardiness in our children, or prevent the habit from forming, the first step is to model punctuality ourselves.

When we are on time for our many commitments- soccer practice, ballet class, movies, place of worship, school- we model the importance of respecting the needs of others. We model self-discipline and responsibility. We model respect for commitments. And we give our children the gift of a good habit, one that will be deeply appreciated by their friends and business associates for the rest of their lives.

When we drop our children off late for school, we are telling them that school is not really that important. That rules are made to be ignored. That their commitment to their teacher and classmates is not really that critical. That being a member of a group does not involve responsibilities to that group. And that the child is really not that important to the success of the group.

School-Smart Parenting Tip

Be on time. Teach your children by example that time commitments are a responsibility that they have, not just to themselves, but to others.

They will then be more inclined to take their school commitments seriously and responsibly, leading to a more enjoyable and productive school experience.

A child raised with a disregard for time commitments is one very much in danger of developing negative attitudes toward societal rules, the expectations of employees, and the needs of others. And the best way to teach our children to be on time is to model that behavior ourselves.

2. Read . . . to yourself and to your children.

When we ourselves read, we model the importance of reading. Let your children see you read. Give them the gift of your modeling the behavior of turning off the television, sitting down in the family room, and spending some time in quality reading.

In addition to modeling the importance of reading, we also model the value of quiet time, of reflection, and of studying when we ourselves read. J. R. R. Tolkein set the stage for the wondrous fantasy world he created very early in *The Hobbit,* his introduction to *The Lord of the Rings* trilogy, by noting that it all takes place "in the quiet of the world, when there was less noise and more green." We've come a long way from that world of quiet and tranquility, but books are one of the best ways to bring us back to it. By reading ourselves, we model that peacefulness, that quiet solitude, that is an essential ingredient of emotional stability.

And read to your children. When should we start reading to our children? As soon as we start speaking to them. For how long should we read to them? For as long as we can hold their attention. At what level should we read to them? Probably about two to three levels above their own reading ability level. (First graders, for example, can probably understand third and fourth grade level books being read to them, even though they may not be able to read them for understanding themselves.)

Reading to our children accomplishes several things. Certainly, our children's reading skills are reinforced when we read to them. They can follow the words with their eyes, say the words to themselves, and read along out loud with us. And if we resist the temptation to make a formal teaching situation out of it- a behavior guaranteed to reduce our children's interest in sitting down with us the next time we try to read to them- the experience will reinforce their developing reading skills.

But much more important, reading to a child offers a very special opportunity to provide one-on-one attention to him, an attention that says "you are significant in my eyes; you are worthy of my time; you deserve this special moment with me." That one-on-one attention, combined with the physical closeness, touch, and warmth that exists in the parent/child reading environment, is powerful medicine, both preventive and curative, for much of what can ail our children. The medical benefits of personal attention, a soothing voice, and physical touch have been understood for centuries and are being rediscovered today even in our medication-biased world.

So take that opportunity to read to your children. Let them have your undivided attention. Let them hear your soothing voice. Let them feel your warmth next to them. They will be physically and emotionally healthier because of it. And, yes, their reading skills will improve.

3. Be discriminating in your TV viewing.

Is television the place where we want our children to find their role models? TV is a wonderful invention, offering entertainment, culture, news, and education to millions who otherwise would never have the opportunity. But as welcome as these benefits are, there are negatives, and we are becoming increasingly aware of them in recent years.

But just complaining about the values our kids are learning from TV is not a very effective approach to the situation- unless, of course, we want to raise children who will address their *own* problems by just complaining about them. Modeling discriminating use of the TV is a much more effective approach.

Some years ago, the late University of Toronto English professor Marshall McLuhan taught us that "the medium is the message." McLuhan's contribution- that the medium itself carries its own message, regardless of the content of the medium- is recognized today as one of the most profound insights of the twentieth century communications revolution. And nowhere does the message of the medium have such a powerful impact on our lives than in television. The rapidly changing, multi-patterned, hyperactive images of television, whether they be projecting the alphabet on *Sesame Street* or a screeching car and the blast of bullets on any number of crime shows, have affected everything in our culture from education (with television being blamed at least in part for the proliferation of Attention Deficit Disorder and hyperactivity diagnoses) to politics (with the art of the sound bite and the advantages of the telegenic candidate).

Our challenge as parents is not to solve the problem by throwing the television away. TV's ability to bring us news, culture, entertainment, and even insight is real and valuable. Our challenge instead is to gain control of television, to be discriminating in its use, to take advantage of the positive opportunities it presents, while

231

remaining conscious of its potential problems. If we want our children to be discriminating in the use of television, we need to model that. We need to keep the TV off unless there is something specific that we want to see. We need to ensure that the TV does not dominate our households.

Probably the least effective response to the television challenge is the example of the home in which the TV is on continuously. It is turned on in the morning to catch the first news of the day, stays on through morning children's shows, on through the soaps and afternoon talk shows, through the early evening news, on to prime time sitcoms, through the evening news, and ending only at the conclusion of the late show. What lessons are we teaching in such a home?

Primarily, we are teaching our children that the television is the ultimate authority in their lives. We are saying that this box, which occupies a place of honor in our family room and is constantly talking to us with words and pictures, is our source for everything important in our lives. Go into any teenager's room and you will immediately learn what is most important to them by what grabs your attention by its place of honor. Maybe it's sports, maybe rock stars, maybe boy friends or girl friends, maybe cars. Whatever it is, it will be evident immediately- on their walls, book shelves, bulletin boards, and mirrors.

The same goes for the home with the continuously running television. That home is screaming out to all who enter it: This machine is the most important thing in this house; whatever you may be concerned about at the moment, whatever you may wish to communicate, whatever need you might have, it is all secondary to the news, sports, sitcoms, and talk shows that this machine is gracing our family with. Children who grow up in such a house, a house in which the parents role model the authority and pre-eminence of the television in their lives, run the risk of becoming shallow thinking, over-stimulated, consumer-driven children whose values are formed by the Roseannes, the Geraldos, and the Al Bundys of the *reel* world, instead of the men and women of the *real* world that we would prefer be instrumental in shaping their values.

Am I being too dramatic here? I don't think so- Is there really any doubt in anybody's mind that TV is the most effective teaching tool that currently exists? And if this is so, by allowing the television to run continuously, do we not thereby allow it to assume the role of our children's primary teacher, teaching them what things are really important, what values we should hold, how we are to treat each other, how we are to talk to each other, how we are to spend our money, how drinking a certain beer will make you young and beautiful and popular? If television was not such a powerful teacher, would companies continue to spend billions yearly on advertising their products to us through that medium?

A guest on *Oprah* once commented that the average child spends approximately ten times as much time in front of the TV than with his mom and forty times as much as with his dad. I can't verify the commentator's statistics, and he gave no source for them himself, but the point is made nonetheless . . . and probably verifiable through our own experience. TV is in fact replacing Mom, Dad, Grandma, Granddad, aunts, uncles, community leaders, and every other possible source of advice, wisdom, and nurturing for our young children. And that is a problem that needs our proactive response.

And yet, having said all the above, it is true that TV can be a positive teacher. There are shows that promote positive values, and VCRs make it possible for us to proactively look for videos with messages that support our own value systems. The choice is really ours: Do we role model discriminating use of the TV by turning it on for a positive program or video, and then turning it back off when it's over, or do we let the TV itself be the role model by keeping it on all day?

Role model responsible use of the television. Role model pre-eminence of your own family values. Role model quiet times. Be discriminating in the use of TV in your home.

School-Smart Parenting Tip

Be discriminating in your TV viewing. Let your own family values have pre-eminence in your family, not the values of TV.

Your children will then face their school years with the strength that comes from clear and constant family values rather than the ever-changing values of the entertainment world. And with their family values to fall back on, they will be more resistant to the peer pressure that will inevitably come their way.

---

4. Project a positive attitude about school.

I once had a meeting with a dad at school to discuss his son's achievement. The dad entered my office, sat down at my conference table, folded his hands sheepishly in his lap, and confessed, "You know, I have to admit that I'm a bit intimidated by being in your office." This man stood six feet, four inches tall and weighed close to three hundred pounds- over a half foot taller and nearly twice my weight. And he was intimidated by *me?*

How we approach our children's school is in large measure a factor of the memories we have from our own schooling. If those memories are positive and empowering, we will communicate that to our children, and they will most likely approach their own schooling in a positive way. If instead, like the dad who was intimidated by being in my office, our memories of school are unpleasant, we will communicate unpleasantness and fearfulness and negativism to our children, and their chances for success and happiness in school are by that degree diminished.

One of the most effective ways to project a positive attitude about school is to use words that suggest that we have positive expectations of what our children will be experiencing. Consider the following three sets of contrasting expressions and ask yourself what perceptions the child will be developing from each:

Expression	Probable Outcome
1. "Oh, you poor dear! How will you ever stay awake from 8:00 until 3:00?" That's too long for a little six-year-old!"	The child will use "I'm too tired" as an excuse for low achievement.

-or-

"Now that you're in the big school, you get to spend the whole day at school. You are getting so big and smart!	The child will see herself as a growing, developing young person anxious to meet new challenges.
2. "Look at all that homework! How do they expect a fourth grader to do that much work!"	The child will develop the habit of complaining as a response to life's challenges, and will learn to see difficulty not as something to overcome but as an excuse for avoidance of responsibilities.

-or-

"That's an impressive homework assignment! They must think very highly of you to expect that much from you."	The child will see himself as becoming a big boy with bigger responsibilities. He may still not appreciate the increased homework load, but he will see it less as a burden and more as an affirmation of his developing maturity.
3. "I was a real cut-up in school. I think I spent more time in the principal's office than in the classroom."	The child will see getting in trouble at school as acceptable behavior.

-or-

"I got in trouble at school a few times too, but I regret it because it hurt me and it hurt the class, and it prevented the teacher from being able to do what she was there to do."

The child will learn that even though he may get in trouble at school from time to time, it is not acceptable because it hurts himself, his classmates, and his teacher. He learns to respect others' needs, not just his own wants.

Many more examples could be given, but these three should suffice to emphasize how the expressions we use affect the way our children see themselves in relation to their schooling. If your memories of schooling are unpleasant, try hard, first, to identify the cause of that unpleasantness and, second, to consciously avoid communicating that unpleasantness to your children. They will encounter their own unpleasantries even in the most positive school environments, so let's not weigh them down with the disadvantage of our own as well.

School-Smart Parenting Tip

Project positive expectations about your children's future. Since we tend to find what we expect to find, positive expectations tend to result in positive outcomes and negative expectations in negative outcomes.

Our children will then be more likely to see their school experiences as leading to productive outcomes and will be more hopeful and optimistic about their futures.

---

5. Show interest in your child's schooling.

Homework is your child's responsibility, not yours. But we can communicate to our children through our active interest that homework is important and relevant. By engaging them in conversation about their homework- "What kinds of things do you have for homework tonight?", "What are your plans for doing your homework tonight?", "Teach me something that you learned in school today."- we show them that we are interested in their school lives and that we support them in their efforts. Further, we model the importance of homework when we make a point of doing our own "homework" in their presence. Whatever the nature of our work during the day, we probably have some work that needs attention after regular hours- I know teachers certainly do!- and doing that work, diligently if not cheerfully, in the presence of our children helps to further communicate the importance of attention to homework.

Schooling is the child's business, just as going to work or organizing the home is our business. But we communicate to the child that we are really interested in his business, in his world, by getting to know the teachers' names, by attending the PTA meetings, by actively involving ourselves in conferences, and by going to the class plays and other school activities. Our physical presence does communicate to our children that they are important enough for us to take time out of our day for them.

Further, we can show real interest by asking questions that invite thoughtful responses. We have all probably learned by our experiences that "Did you have a good day?" rarely invites more than a grunt in response. But when we shift to "So what's one interesting thing that happened in school today?," we help focus the child's thought processes to a specific event, making it more likely that he will respond meaningfully.

Other expressions that help our children focus their thoughts, resulting in a greater probability of thoughtful responses, are: "What is one new thing you learned in school today?", "Teach me one thing you learned new in school today", "Tell me one good thing that happened in school today", and even "Tell me one thing that didn't work out so well in school today." (Never use that last one in isolation. Follow it up with "Now tell me one *good* thing that happened in school today" so the child doesn't get focused on the negative. One good reason to ask a child to talk about one thing that didn't work out so well is to communicate to him that we know that life isn't always perfect, and that we would like to support him in his challenges. But it's important to follow this up with an expression of positive expectations so that they learn that they do have the ability to influence life for the better.)

By being physically present at school when it is appropriate and important to do so we communicate real interest in the schooling part of our children's lives. By talking to them and listening to them about their school experiences, we reinforce that interest as well as give them opportunities to verbalize their thoughts, explore their perceptions, and validate their conclusions. And if we combine this with respect for the privacy they will from time to time need regarding their schooling, we will make communication with us a safe and supportive experience.

6. Model problem-solving skills.

An excellent rule in dealing with adults and children alike is "Always look for solutions, not for blame." Our usual first impulse when something goes wrong is to look for blame: Who did that? Who is responsible for that? Whose dumb idea was that?

But looking for solutions rather than blame shifts the focus to the 'what' rather than the 'who,' thereby freeing all involved to stand back and objectively review the situation. Looking for solutions rather than blame places no one on the defensive and no one on the offensive. It unites all in a common mission, looking for a solution to the problem.

How best to model that at home? There are numerous ways to define a problem solving process. One of the most effective is the EIAG process introduced by Steve Glenn and Jane Nelsen in *Raising Self-Reliant Children in a Self-Indulgent World*. EIAG, pronounced "eye-ag," is an acronym for Experience-Identify-Analyze-Generalize. Simply stated, EIAG is an invitation to see our experiences as opportunities for growth rather than as excuses for blaming, criticizing, fault-finding, or discounting. It is an invitation to take every experience we have and every experience our children have and explore what happened, why it happened that way, and, if the experience was negative, what we can do to ensure a better outcome next time (or, if the experience was positive, what we can do to transfer what we learned here to other experiences we might have.)

If I can sit down with my son after he has failed a test and engage him in dialogue about what went wrong, why it went wrong, and how he can prepare to do better next time, I will, through the EIAG process, demonstrate interest in what is going on in his life, show respect for his own ideas about how to improve, and support him in his efforts. An effective approach, one that avoids lecturing and blaming, might be along the lines of the following:

Matthew: "That stupid Mr. Harmon, he doesn't know how to teach anything. Everybody in the class failed the social studies test."

Dad: "Does that mean that you failed the social studies test?"

Matthew: "Yeah, everybody did. He doesn't know how to teach."

Dad: "What did you get on the test?"

Matthew: "A 52. I told you, everybody failed."

Dad: "How did you prepare for the test?"

Matthew: "We didn't prepare for the test. That's the point. He just announced that there would be a test and never went over what was going to be on it."

Dad: "You mean it was a pop test?"

Matthew: "No, he told us yesterday that there would be a test on Chapter 6, but he didn't review what was going to be on it."

Dad: "Oh, I get it now. You knew that there would be a test, but Mr. Harmon didn't spend any class time reviewing what exactly would be on it. He just told you that you had to study Chapter 6."

Matthew: "Yeah, and that's not fair. Mrs. Wolfe always spends a whole class period going over what will be on her tests the day before. That way we know exactly what to study. Mr. Harmon justs tells us to study the chapter."

Dad: "Why do you think he does it that way?"

Matthew: "Probably because he wants us all to fail!"

Dad: "Maybe so. But what other reasons might he have than just trying to ruin your life?"

Matthew: "I don't know. Maybe he thinks his precious class time is too important to waste on test preparation. Maybe he just likes to tell all his corny stories about history and can't tell them if we have to spend time reviewing for tests. I don't know."

Dad: "I thought you enjoyed his stories."

Matthew: "Yeah, sometimes they're interesting. But I still wish he'd spend some class time reviewing for the tests."

Dad: "I can understand that. It would make it easier. But since he probably won't do that, what ideas do you have for doing better on the next test?"

Matthew: "I guess I need to read the chapter over again. Maybe compare what I've read to the class notes. He did tell us to pay particular attention to what he talks about in class, that those things would be the major emphasis on his tests. But it's still not fair."

Dad: "Good idea. Oh, by the way, how many kids really did fail the test?"

Matthew: "The whole class. That's my story and I'm sticking to it. I'm going to go study for the next test now. Bye."

As demonstrated above, EIAG is more an attitude that a technique. More than reduce the conversation to a formulaic "What happened, why did it happen, and what can you do to fix it?," Dad is trying to get into his son's world, show real interest in what happened, listen to his thoughts and perceptions, empathize with his struggles, and offer guidance. By asking questions that help him identify what happened (he failed the test), analyze why it happened that way (not having reviewed for the test in school, it was necessary to do more serious review at home, which hadn't been done), and what he could do next time (pay more attention to the class notes, reread the chapter), Dad is allowing his son to experience how he can influence his world and make effective judgments. Yes, it all takes a bit more time than offering the standard lecture, but how much more effective it is in the long run!

7. Teach respect by being respectful.

Have you ever heard someone say that children need to *earn* our respect? Let's all agree to bury that attitude for good. No one needs to earn anyone else's respect. Respect should be a given. It should be unqualified, given unconditionally. Respect should be something we are *owed,* by virtue of our humanity, not *earned* as a result of our satisfactorily living up to someone else's expectations.

We effectively model respect by sincerely showing that respect to our children and to everyone we meet. When Mom is shopping with her daughter, she models respect in how she speaks to the salesperson. When she takes her son to work, she models respect in how she speaks to her associates, particularly to those who work under her. When Dad is at his daughter's soccer game, he models respect in how he speaks to the coaches and referees. Simply put, we model respect continuously through our daily interactions with others. And our children learn respect from what they observe and receive from us.

There is one particular problem regarding respect that I have encountered with some frequency and that needs to be addressed here. It is the issue of how spouses treat each other and how that example translates to the child's perception of the teacher. I have no data on this, just my own observations, but I do suspect strongly that a dad's lack of respectfulness for his wife will tend to translate to his son's lack of respectfulness for his female teachers. If our sons are raised in a home in which the most significant member of the female sex is treated disrespectfully, with little regard for her opinions, feelings, capabilities, and needs, we run the risk that this attitude will be universalized for all women, something that becomes quite significant in the world of teaching. Not only does the mom have to suffer the indignities of disrespectful treatment, but so too will the teachers. (All of this applies as well to young girls and male teachers, of course.) When we deal with our spouse, we need to be aware that our children will be learning from that interaction, and they will take what they learn and apply it in their own lives . . . for good or for ill.

8. Demonstrate respect for those in the teaching profession.

In 1995, an article in the *Dallas Morning News* relayed the story of how several Dallas Independent School District administrators, found guilty of some minor infractions, were, as discipline, 'demoted' to the status of teachers. The clear impression given was that teaching was considered by those in personnel decision-making positions at DISD to be a lower status position, the demotion to which would be understood as discipline for the infractions. As you might imagine, the school district was hit with a barrage of criticism, largely from offended teachers but also from many parents and even school administrators at this slight to the teaching profession.

And rightly so. As a school administrator myself, I am very well aware of the decision-making powers that I have that can affect, positively or negatively, the future of our children's schooling. But

244

with the exception of their parents, no one has greater influence on the lives of young children than their teachers. And being married to a kindergarten teacher, I can attest to the fact that there are no harder working people on earth. Teachers are over-worked, under-paid, and under-appreciated, and it's a national scandal. When men who spend their lives hitting a piece of cowhide with a stick and running around in a circle to celebrate are paid more in a year than the average teacher will make in a lifetime, we have serious problems with national priorities. And because we tend to measure not only success but also dignity and worth in terms of income level, we must be vigilant that our children do not perceive teachers to occupy a lower level of society because they are not compensated like other professionals. (The same can be said, by the way, of the over-worked, under-paid, and under-appreciated in any number of other helping professions, not to mention numerous service positions, in our society.)

Every job, every occupation, every profession is worthy of dignity and respect. But the extensive and long-lasting influence of the teacher on the child compels us here to reflect on the importance of raising our children with a special respect for teachers. Anything we can do to raise our children to not measure people in terms of their financial success is critical . . . and difficult, given the attention the media places on success. If we raise our children in homes that emphasize the importance of contribution over individual achievement, affirmation and celebration of their own interests instead of pressure to buy into the agenda of the media, and emotional stability rather than continuous pressure to join this club, participate in that activity, try out for this team, be the best, etc., we will have gone a long way toward placing emphasis on healthier

245

priorities. And if we demonstrate respectfulness toward teachers ourselves, in our words and in our interactions with them, we will complete the picture.

School-Smart Parenting Tip

Demonstrate respect for the teaching profession. Let your children know that you believe that teaching is a highly valued skill and that teachers are dedicated individuals committed to their students.

Our children will then be more willing to learn from their teachers and to respectfully and cooperatively work with them, leading to a more pleasant school experience for all.

We will encounter some really effective teachers in our children's school years, just as we did in our own. And we will also encounter some ineffective ones. But let's not prejudice our children from the onset against teachers and teaching by communicating our disagreements or by emphasizing society's misplaced values.

9. Teach family work by doing chores yourself.

The emergency family meeting that Carol called not so long ago was a healthy reality check for me. The truth is that I was not doing my fair share around the house, which resulted in several problems.

First, Carol was overburdened with work and growing increasingly resentful of my failure to step up to the plate and contribute. Second, the house was not becoming as well organized or as clean as it might otherwise be. And third, and most important, our children were not seeing the model of a dad who pitches in around the house doing the mundane chores just like everybody else. And since boys tend to develop their interpersonal relationship skills and sense of responsibilities more from their dad than from their mom (and *vice versa* for girls), this negative lesson would weigh more heavily on my son. In short, I was running the risk that Thomas would grow up to believe that assisting with the family chores was not his responsibility, not part of the lessons of life that he would receive from his dad.

The reorganization of the family chores turned out to be a positive lesson for all of us. We came to appreciate the hard work that everybody does, we became more tolerant of times when chores were not completed exactly as expected, and we grew in respect for the appearance of our home. In fact, it helped all of us see that it was truly *our* home.

So, Dad, pitch in and be a model for your children. We teach not through sermons but through experiences, and the most effective teaching experience is that of our own modeling.

10. Listen to your kids.

Understand that although younger children may tell you everything that's going on in their lives, older ones may put up a "No Trespassing" sign, keeping their thoughts very much to themselves and resenting your "intrusions." In both cases, our listening skills are challenged. In the first, we are challenged to drop our agenda, put down the newspaper, turn off the TV, and give the child undivided attention.

But in the second, our listening skills are challenged just as much, if not more so. You may be thinking, How can my listening skills be challenged when she's not saying anything? But is it really that she is not saying anything, or is it that we are not hearing what she *is* saying?

I once returned from a speaking engagement out of town to be met at the airport by Carol alone. It was a week night, so I knew that Thomas was working, but where was Jennifer, fifteen years old at the time? Previously, Jennifer would always be there, waiting for me. Actually more than waiting, she would be excitedly anticipating my arrival. I had come to expect that once I exited the plane and entered the passenger tunnel I would soon see Jennifer, peering down the corridor yelling "Daddy, daddy!" But today, no Jennifer.

When I arrived home, still no Jennifer. She was there, but she was in her room, listening to her music, talking on the telephone, probably doing her homework all at the same time. She knew I had arrived, but she elected to stay in her room and ignore Daddy's homecoming.

What was she saying? Volumes. First of all, she was *not* saying, "Daddy, I'm too busy and self-absorbed to come out and greet you, much less waste my time driving to the airport to pick you up; I'll come out and say hello when I'm good and ready." But I certainly could have interpreted it that way, and when she finally exited her room I could have retaliated with, "Well, thanks a lot for giving me some time, Little Miss Self-Absorbed!" And the rest of the evening would be downhill from there, not to mention our relationship.

What Jennifer *was* saying was, "Daddy, I'm fifteen now and I'm becoming a different person from the little girl you knew before. It's important to me that you see me that way. I will always miss you when you go out of town, and I will always celebrate your arrival, but I need to show you in this little way that I am growing up and developing interests of my own- including this other male person in my life who I have been talking to on the phone for the past hour!- and I hope you appreciate and respect that."

I suspected as much when I saw no Jennifer at the airport, and so when I returned home I simply threw my bags on the living room floor and crashed on the sofa to chat with Carol. About a half hour later, Jennifer emerged from her room, sat down on the sofa next to me, and said, "Hi, Daddy, I missed you." Then she put her head on my shoulder.

Listening to our kids often means practicing the restraint of saying nothing and just waiting instead. Sometimes our kids don't talk to us because we are monopolizing the agenda, or just invading their space with too many questions: "How was school today?" "Do you have any homework?" "Did you do your chores yet?" Effective listening often results from our silence, which allows the child to advance *her* agenda and tell us what's on *her* mind. And if we follow her agenda and resist the temptation to return to our own, we will be modeling effective and respectful listening, the foundation of effective and respectful communication.

11. Husbands, love your wives; wives, love your husbands.

It has been said that the greatest gift a father can give his children is to love his wife. Likewise, the greatest gift a mother can give her children is to love her husband. And no greater thing can be modeled than love itself.

Philosophers throughout the centuries have tried in vain to define love. Books have been written on the meaning of love, the challenge of love, the metaphysics of love, and, of course, the sexuality of love. Each of us has his own definition, and mine is simple: Love is nothing more than "a whole lotta like."

When you love someone, you like them "a whole lot." You want to be with them, and you respect their occasional need to be alone. You enjoy their conversation, and you respect their need for quiet. You listen to them patiently, and you offer help when it is requested. In short, you treat them respectfully.

I have very few clear memories about my childhood other than the general perception that it was a happy one. But one of the memories I do have goes back to watching television at about seven or eight years of age. The show was a fifties version of today's talk show, and the participants were a man and a woman debating the value of fighting- verbal fighting, not physical fighting- in marriage. There was an audience present, and the emcee was doing his best to involve them by asking provocative questions that would evoke impassioned responses. And he was succeeding.

The woman argued for the benefit of a good fight. She talked about how important it is to shout out your anger and say whatever's on your mind and get it all off your chest. She bragged about how she calls her husband every name she can think of during one of their "good fights," and how he does the same back, and how the neighbors can all hear them, and how funny it all is. And she concluded by saying that there's nothing like the feeling you get when you make up after a real shouting exchange.

This lady looked the part- the tough-as-nails, all-American woman with a tongue that could kill and a heart of gold. She had the audience on her side throughout, and she was clearly the emcee's favorite as well. I'll bet her name was Marge.

The man, for his part, was trying to get a word in edgewise in support of the relationship in which shouting had no place. When he did get an opening, he reasoned painstakingly for respectfulness in relationships, for honest but dignified exchanges of feelings, for the household in which peacefulness, not warring factions, was the norm. I remember that he looked distinctly un-American (for the fifties): slight, thin, with a goatee . . . having somewhat of a foreign appearance. (And knowing what we now know about the less-than-pure television industry of the fifties- remember the movie *Quiz Show?*- I have no doubt that he was chosen for that part in the debate precisely *because* of the way he looked. I don't remember his name, but we can be sure it wasn't Norm or Harry or Al.)

I can remember sitting there watching the show and feeling sorry for the man. He was trying so hard to infuse reason and dignity and respectfulness into the situation, but he just kept being shouted down by 'Marge' and the audience. A good fight won out over reasoned discussion. A free flowing exchange of animosities won out over respectfulness. Making up after a "good fight" won out over the relationship that grows through continuing courtesies, occasional slip-ups, and renewed commitments.

I believed then, and I believe now, that the man in that debate spoke for the higher way. Yes, we will blow it from time to time. But let's not rationalize that into the norm. Do our children experience love when we parents talk to each other? Do they see love in our daily interactions? Do they sense love and respect and emotional stability in our relationship?

The renowned spiritualist and anthropologist Teilhard de Chardin once wrote that someday, after we have conquered the sun and the moon, the tides and the seas, we shall harness for man the energies of love, and then, for the second time in the history of the world, we will have discovered fire. In our own little worlds, let's harness the energies of love and discover, and reveal to our children, that fire. Let's strive to make those occasional unpleasant moments in our married life the exceptions we regret rather than the norm of our relationship. Let's give our kids the model of the emotionally stable married life.

12. Be spiritual persons.

If love is difficult to define, even more so is spirituality. Not long ago I had the opportunity to hike to the top of Guadalupe Peak, the highest point in Texas at 8700 feet, with my son. Now 8700 feet is a mere foothill by Rocky Mountain standards, but in Texas it's the best we've got, and, in fact, it was a fairly challenging hike for a couple of lowlanders. And when we got to the top and looked down on the great West Texas desert below, all I could think of was the incredible wonder of creation, its beauty and majesty, its awesomeness. I stood there on the top of Guadalupe Peak, turned in all directions to get the full scope and range of beauty below me, and kept repeating, over and over again, the single word "awesome." For me, at that moment, spirituality was on the top of Guadalupe Peak.

I would define spirituality in terms of awesomeness, and I encounter awesomeness in creation. My own personal journey of discovery as I encounter this awesomeness leads me to the recognition of a Creator, who must be very great and very good to produce something of the majesty of Guadalupe Peak. And my further reflections, with the support of a religious tradition that dates back several thousand years, lead me to understand this Creator as one who loves every man, woman, and child unconditionally, and I take great comfort in that.

I also see this Creator as the ultimate role model for mankind, particularly in regard to this example of unconditional love. And my personal faith helps me flesh all this out in very specific ways, leading me to certain specific beliefs, to an appreciation and growing understanding of right and wrong, to a predeliction to service, and to rituals and traditions that support me in my spiritual journey.

But what is important here is not the specific faith that we may have but the simple recognition that there is something greater than ourselves that helps us see more clearly who we are, why we are, and how we are to relate to each other. It is important that we share this recognition with our children. It is important that we give them the gift of the rituals and traditions that define our understanding of spirituality. It is important that they grow to see themselves as part of a rich heritage that helps to give their lives meaning and purpose.

Finally, be a model, not a critic. This may be the best summation of all that has been written in this chapter. Be a model, not a critic. Teach by doing, not by critiquing. Don't talk about, just do it. And our kids will learn the importance of doing, of acting, of taking the necessary steps, not just talking about it. Their schooling, as well as all aspects of their lives, will be enhanced because of it.

PART THREE

PARENTS AND TEACHERS:
TEAMING UP FOR THE SAKE OF OUR CHILDREN

In our final three chapters, we close out our look at raising children for success and happiness in school by encouraging parents and teachers to team up for the sake of our children. In Chapter 8, we present the "No-Rescue Contract," a vehicle for encouraging dialogue between the parent and the child, the parent and the teacher, and the child and the teacher. The "No-Rescue Contract" in effect asks the question: "What am I willing to let go of so that my child will be allowed to grow in self-reliance and responsibility?"

In Chapter 9, we remind ourselves that no person is an island and that effective parenting need not- indeed, *can not*- take place without a network of supportive individuals. Schools across America are becoming more and more conscious of this and have responded with a focus on the family demonstrated by everything from renewed calls for parental involvement to the sponsoring of formal parenting classes.

And in Chapter 10, we close with a word to teachers (but also for parents) in which we offer suggestions for promoting Contribution, Affirmation, and Emotional Stability in the classroom, just as parents will be striving to do the same on the home front. It is our goal that all of us- parents and teachers- will be "on the same page" in our efforts to create the environment most conducive for happy and successful schooling.

CHAPTER 8

THE NO-RESCUE CONTRACT

Mrs. Redbird loved her child so much she could not stand it to push
him out of the nest. In the name of love, her child never
learned to fly.

-Positive Discipline Study Guide, Jane Nelsen

Before the Pilgrims disembarked from the Mayflower to plant their
feet on Plymouth Rock, they wrote up a contract to facilitate and
determine the terms of their interactions and governance. The
Mayflower Compact, as it came to be called, holds center stage in
our history not so much for what it says, but for the precedence it
set, a precedence that has become integral to American culture,
namely, to write things down and affix our signatures to them as a
sign of commitment. The several state constitutions, the Declaration
of Independence, the United States Constitution, and the
constitutions of dozens of nations that have come into being since
our own and have emulated our need to "write it down," all attest to
the power of the signed statement.

The signed statement in the form of a contract has also been
popular in business settings, with the signatures confirming that all
parties are in agreement to what has been written down. Many

parents have emulated this in parent/child contracts that spell out the rules and consequences regarding curfews, use of the car, chores, etc., with both the parents and the child affixing their signatures to signify commitment to the agreement. The "No-Rescue Contract," designed specifically to encourage effective parenting in school situations, carries with it a similar degree of seriousness and commitment for the participating parent, child, and school.

What is the "No-Rescue Contract"? It is simply a statement, to be signed by the parent and the student, committing both to strive to work together to avoid rescuing and to promote self-reliance and responsibility.

Why a "No-Rescue Contract"? Because rescuing may very well be the most common barrier we parents erect to our children's development as capable students. And because the written contract, sealed with our signatures, is the means through which our culture attaches seriousness to commitments.

Like the mom who rushes to school to deliver a forgotten lunch or the dad who time after time bails his daughter out of some disciplinary situation she has gotten herself into, all of us parents face the temptation to rescue, probably on a daily basis. And the temptation is a powerful one, presenting itself, as it does, as a test of our love. If we love our children, the temptation suggests, we will change our daily schedule to deliver their forgotten lunch, lest they go hungry; if we love them, we will protect them from the logical consequences of their behavior. So goes the temptation.

Shortly after we had offered the "No-Rescue Contract" at school, a mom complained to me that she did not agree with it and therefore she chose not to participate in it. I reminded her that that was fine, that participation in the program was voluntary, that we meant it only as a vehicle through which parents and their children might discuss the importance of personal responsibility, etc. But then I asked, just out of curiosity, what exactly in the "No-Rescue Contract" did she not feel comfortable with. "Well," she replied, "the fact is I *enjoy* being there for my son. I *enjoy* bringing his lunch to school when he forgets it. I *enjoy* dressing him in the morning. I *want* to be there side by side with him if he has problems at school." And who of us can not empathize with a mother's strong desire to provide for her son?

But let's be honest here. Whose needs is this mom focusing on, her son's or her own? Whose needs is she really addressing? And what needs of the son are being met by a parent who insists on preventing him from discovering ways to work through life's difficulties?

It is so important to remember here that it will never be safer for a child to make mistakes, nor will it ever be easier for a child to learn from those mistakes, than it is in those early elementary school years. If we can allow those mistakes to happen- forgotten lunch, mismatched clothing, forgotten homework- and then respectfully and supportively work *with* the child, helping him to reach his own conclusions on how best to avoid the problem next time, we will be doing a much greater service for him than stepping in and rescuing him. Asking those simple exploring questions- What happened with your lunch today, son? What caused you to forget to put it in your backpack? What ideas do you have for helping yourself remember to put it in your backpack tomorrow?- shows far more respectfulness for the child than continually bailing him out, which only calls into question his progress as a capable person.

The "No-Rescue Contract" was designed to provide the supportive, encouraging framework within which parents and children might discuss the reasons for avoiding rescuing and exploring alternatives to it. It is recommended that schools individualize the contract to meet their unique needs, communicate clearly at parent club meetings the purpose of the contract, and encourage parents to sit down with their children to discuss its implications and, if they choose to participate, sign the contract with them. (I like to provide two copies of the contract for each child, one to keep at home and one to return to school to be maintained "on file.")

What are the elements of the "No-Rescue Contract"? In the example on pages 264-265, the following is included:

• a heading noting the school's name

• a preamble that clearly states the purpose of the contract, namely, to underscore our desire to provide our children with opportunities to grow in self-reliance and personal responsibility

• an affirmation of our children as capable, significant young people who can influence the direction their futures will take and the world in which they will live

• a recognition of our own role as parents and the distinctiveness of that role from that of teachers, combined with a pledge to be supportive of one another

• a commitment by the young person to take the role of student seriously

• a commitment to mutual respectfulness

• a place for the signatures of parents and child

If your children's school does not yet take advantage of the "No-Rescue Contract," bring the idea to their attention. Make it a project of your parents' club. Involve teachers and administrators in the formulation of the contract, and encourage participation through education on its merits and clear communication about its purpose.

Have panel discussions involving counselors, teachers, parents, administrators, and, if appropriate, students. Bring in speakers to address the subject. Provide workshops that allow participants to experience alternatives to rescuing, such as allowing natural consequences, fashioning logical consequences, using the what/why/how process, and respecting our children's capabilities.

263

Central Elementary School

No-Rescue Contract

In recognition of the understanding that our ultimate responsibility as parents is to work ourselves out of the job, and desirous of raising our children as self-reliant young people who will grow to understand that their efforts do have consequences, we hereby pledge to try our best to support them in those efforts by:

☐ affirming them as capable young people who can dress themselves, do their own homework, pack their own bags, find their own way to their desks, and deal with forgotten homework, supplies, and lunches on their own;

☐ affirming them as significant young people who are true contributors in our family life, not just objects of our direction or recipients of our rescuing, who can, with our patient assistance, come up with ideas on their own on how best to do their homework, how best to ensure that their clothes are ready in the morning, and how best to remember to bring all their supplies to school; and

☐ affirming them as young people of influence who can make decisions on their own, experience the consequences of those decisions, and work with us to grow in an understanding of why their particular efforts yielded the results that they experienced.

As parents, we realize that it is far more important that our children make mistakes from which they can learn than that we always look good. We pledge to work with them in both their successes and "near-successes" so that they can learn from them. We understand that just as the teachers do not need to get involved in disciplinary matters that take place at home, we do not need to get involved in disciplinary matters that take place at school. The teachers do not need to add consequences to at-home infractions, and we parents do not need to add consequences to at-school infractions. We simply need to support each other in our efforts and dialogue with our children to help them gain a greater understanding of what happened, why it happened that way, and what they can do next time to ensure the best possible outcome.

As students, we pledge to do our very best at all times, to take responsibility for our behavior and our assignments, and to work cooperatively with our teachers and fellow students.

And together, we parents and students pledge to treat each other respectfully at all times, understanding that respect is not something that we need to earn but is, rather, owed to every man, woman, and child unconditionally.

Parent signature(s) _____   Student

Signature _____

Date _____

In short, let the "No-Rescue Contract" become the impetus for a dialogue among all players in the school community- parents, teachers, students, counselors, administrators-, a dialogue leading to more capable, responsible, and respectful partners in the education business.

CHAPTER 9

NETWORKING FOR SUCCESSFUL PARENTING

No man is an island,
entire of itself.

-John Donne

Parenting is the most important job you will ever have. It is also the toughest job you will ever have. To maximize our potential for success, and to make the job so much more pleasant, it is helpful to remember that no person is an island and that, therefore, we are called upon to involve others in our struggles.

No person was meant to live alone, and no parent was meant to work through the challenges of parenting in isolation from others. We are social creatures who need the company of others to survive. We need communication, touch, support, and empathy. We need others to celebrate with us our triumphs and mourn with us our defeats. We need to know that we are all in the same boat, and we need to learn from each other how to make that boat sail more smoothly.

All of this has become so much more critical in the world that has emerged during the last fifty years. In 1940, just before World War II, two out of every three American families had a grandparent living with them. Today it is two out of 100. In 1940, two out of every three American families had an in-house consultant, an in-house mentor, an in-house trainer, and, most important, an adult role model who always had time for the kids. Further, in 1940 Mom and Dad were complemented by a vast network of aunts and uncles and friends, in addition to Grandma and Granddad, who shared the same values and traditions as they did and who were always there to support them in their efforts. Today, due largely to the mobility of our culture, such a natural network of friends and relatives is very much the exception. Our challenge then is to, first, recognize what we have lost, and, second, seek ways to compensate for it. If we do not have the natural support system for our parenting efforts that a previous culture provided, we must then create one.

This is why we need to proactively seek out opportunities to build community in our neighborhoods, in our schools, in our places of worship. We must seek out support groups and involve ourselves in opportunities to enhance our parenting skills. We need to share our struggles with others, listen empathically to their struggles, and grow in understanding through the process. We need to actively create situations in which we can build relationships in settings that are safe, supportive, encouraging, and non-threatening.

School-Smart Parenting Tip

Build support systems for your devleoping parenting skills.
In doing so, you will not only help yourself, but you will
also be teaching your children the importance of cooperation
and building relationships with others, valuable lessons
for schooling and life.

My own experience in conducting classes that support parenting skills through the Developing Capable People program has taught me that we parents typically follow specific stages of awareness. Initially, we are looking for quick answers, something to "fix" the problem, tricks that will make our children behave right now and bring normalcy to our lives. And, sadly, some parents withdraw from the process once they learn that any honest parenting approach demands something more than quick, easy answers. If it has taken the child and the parent living together for five, seven, ten, or fifteen years to develop the current relationship that they have, it will surely take more than a quick fix to improve that relationship. And improvement is ongoing: Our relationships with the significant persons in our lives will change, decline, improve, and develop throughout our lives. Indeed, the wonder of relationship is its dynamism; it is ever changing, ever growing.

So the very notion of a quick fix is foreign to the notion of growth in interpersonal relationships. But once a commitment is made to become part of the ongoing process of support, a second stage of development is entered. Once parents commit themselves to learning ways to provide opportunities for their children to become capable, significant young people who can make decisions that influence their world, a realization occurs that makes the rest of the process possible. It is the realization that I cannot help others unless I first help myself. Like the flight attendant who reminds us that if we are to save our child during oxygen deprivation we must first apply the oxygen mask to ourselves, then to the child, we enter a second stage of effectiveness when we realize that we first must see *ourselves* as capable and significant people if we want our children to perceive themselves as such. When that is realized, the

269

importance of taking the time for sharing with others, for taking the time to become part of support groups, for taking the time for self-renewal becomes very clear. Continuing growth in awareness is now possible.

Jon, married and with three children ages two through seven, came to my Developing Capable People class several years ago. From the very beginning he made it clear that he wanted no part of this parenting stuff, that he had so much better to do than spend nine weeks listening to a bunch of women (he was the only male in a group of eleven), and that the only reason he had signed up was because his wife had insisted upon it. She had gone through the course a year before and really wanted to provide a united front for their children. Jon, in short, was my challenge for the course.

Other than making the reluctance of his presence known to all other class participants, Jon did not participate in the first class. When he came to the second class, he came without his "Participant's Workbook," a journaling companion to the course that is essential for full participation. Neither did he have a pencil or pen. Needless to say, he hadn't done the prescribed readings. I avoided the temptation to ask if his dog had eaten his homework.

Throughout the class, he looked for every opportunity he could to find the one point that he could disagree with that would allow him to justify his rejection of the entire course. I call this attitude the "exclusionary temptation," that unfortunate tendency we all find ourselves in from time to time to look for that one flaw, that one point of disagreement, that one slight shade of difference that will allow us to entirely reject a person's beliefs, his values, his perceptions, his contributions, his very self. In contrast to the "exclusionary temptation" is the "inclusionary invitation," through

270

which we are encouraged to look for that one point of agreement, that one point of convergence, that one point of connectedness through which we can include the other in our lives and say yes to his beliefs, values, perceptions, and personhood. Clearly, Jon was suffering from a bad case of the "exclusionary temptation."

Now it's very important in these situations to avoid challenging the other person head on. Challenge is an important step in the development of our skills, but it is good to remember that support must precede any challenge we offer, and the perception of support by the other person will take time.

So I refused to take the bait that Jon would throw out to me. I tried as hard as I could to affirm his opinions and perceptions, and I modeled, as best I could, the "inclusionary invitation" by showing him how his contributions contributed to the discussion. Further, and more important, the other participants in the class modeled this for Jon by refusing to encourage his isolation and working hard to affirm him. In fact, Jon became a class project, a very therapeutic exercise for the other participants through which they could externalize their own challenges in Jon, work through them by affirming and assisting him, and thereby solve their own problems in the process.

Interestingly, Jon came to every class and he came on time, often the first person there. Frequently, he came without his journal and/or without a pencil or pen, but he always came. When discussion would take place on the readings assigned during the week, Jon would take delight in announcing that he didn't have time to do the readings, which, of course, didn't stop him from offering contrary opinions to every point brought up by the others. But gradually we noticed that his opposition was being offered with less

271

and less enthusiasm as the classes progressed.

During the opening activities of the seventh class session, activities during which the class participants share with each other their successes and "near successes" of the previous week in terms of the specific goal they had set for themselves, Jon surprised all of us by announcing that he would like to share his own experiences of the week first. He told us how his daughter came up to him while he was watching television and sat down next to him on the couch and started poking him in the arm. He told us that he started to respond in anger to her disruption but something, he didn't know what or why, caused him to stop, to ask himself why she was poking him, and to make the decision to turn off the television and turn, instead, to his daughter. He then told us that he had the longest conversation with his daughter that he had ever had in his life, that she spontaneously kissed him when it was time to go and do her homework, and that he had immediately reached for his journal to jot down the thoughts that were overcoming him just then. Then, in front of all of us, he lowered his head and sobbed.

Needless to say, it was a very powerful moment for all of us in the class. It was the moment that cemented the relationships that were forming during the nine-week course. It was the moment of awareness for Jon, and for all of us, that no person is an island, that only through building relationships and building community will we grow as persons. It was a moment celebrated by hugs all around.

Without the course, without the support of the class participants, Jon would most likely never have questioned the road he was taking. But his involvement in the process of learning how to develop more capable young people, reluctant though it was, provided the opening through which other people could enter his

272

life, demonstrate their support for his efforts, empathize with his struggles, offer suggestions for improvement, and provide the incentive to stop and question himself at a very critical point in his life. Jon had a long way to go, but it is no exaggeration to say that on that day he took the first step.

The importance of involving other people in your life to offer support for your struggles in raising your children for success and happiness in school cannot be overemphasized. When we join with others, formally in class settings or just informally in social settings, we give ourselves the gift of another's point of view, of another's perceptions, of another's experiences. We really do come to see that we are all in the same boat, and we really do learn from each other how to make that boat sail more smoothly.

So take the initiative. Check out your school, place of worship, or business and locate the various parent groups that are available. Many school systems now have pre-school PTA's in addition to the regular school PTA's to encourage involvement of younger parents and provide them opportunities to come together and form communities. Places of worship across the religious spectrum are growing in awareness of the importance of supporting family life-something that, by the way, is resulting in the breaking down of old barriers between the various religions as this new shared need is being discovered-, and many of them are offering courses in parenting. Businesses throughout our country are realizing that the most frequent reasons for employee absences and stress on the job are problems in the home, and they are beginning to offer parenting classes and counseling services for them.

The opportunities to network with other parents are there. We only need to seek them out. And by doing so and taking an active part we not only help ourselves and our children, but we provide incentives for others to get involved in the process of growth as well. We benefit, our family benefits, our community benefits, and our world benefits. Which is as it should be, because no person is an island.

CHAPTER 10

A WORD TO TEACHERS

"Why not be a teacher? You'd be a fine teacher. Perhaps even a great one."
"And if I was, who would know it?"
"You, your pupils, your friends, God. Not a bad public, that."

-dialogue between Sir Thomas More and Richard Rich,
from Robert Bolt's *A Man for All Seasons*

Talk to any veteran kindergarten teacher about how children have changed over the years and you'll get an earful. If that teacher has been around for twenty years or more, you will no doubt hear something like the following: "Back then, the children would mind. If I told them to be quiet for circle time, they would be quiet. If I told them to listen to me, they would listen to me. If I said no, they accepted it. Today, many of them do whatever they want, whenever they want. I don't know if it's television, day care, affluence, not enough adults in their lives, or what, but kids today are definitely different."

And no doubt we have all heard the old timer's lament: "When I got disciplined at school, that was the easy part. The hard part came when I got home. The whippin' I got from my dad for misbehavin'

275

in school was far worse than what I got from the teacher. Today, if the teacher disciplines a kid, the parents sue the teacher!" I've always believed that there is much more anecdote than actuality to that statement, but the sentiment remains true nonetheless.

Yes, kids today are definitely different. We've all heard about the so-called list of "Concerns and Worries" that plagued teachers in the fifties as reported on an evening news show several years back. The list included such items as gum-chewing, speaking out without raising hands, being late for classes, and the like. The news report compared this to a list of concerns of teachers in the eighties, which we could now extend to the nineties and beyond- drugs, sex, violence, and the absence of any accepted ethical code of behavior. Whether there really was a list of "Concerns and Worries" drawn up in the fifties has been subject to debate, but that issue is irrelevant. Except in isolated schools such as the one portrayed in the fifties movie *The Blackboard Jungle,* drugs, sex, and violence in the schools were rarely concerns of American teachers back then; they are very much our concerns today.

Teachers, this chapter is for you. Up until this point, we have addressed parents, with the understanding that the most important thing we parents can do to ensure success and happiness in school for our children is to provide an environment conducive to Contribution, Affirmation, and Emotional Stability. I do not believe that there is anything more important than this. I *do* believe that if we parents focus less on the kind of school we need for our children, less on the philosophy of the curriculum of the school, less on the credentials of the teachers, less on the part of town the school is located in, and less on the ethnic make-up of the students, and focus instead on our own parenting- specifically, ensuring

276

opportunities for chores, showing real interest in our children's lives, and providing emotional stability in the home- then we will be doing the best that we can for our children. Capable, responsible, and effective people focus not on what others need to change but on what they themselves need to change in their own lives.

The question for us teachers now is this: How can we support the efforts of parents to provide an environment of Contribution, Affirmation, and Emotional Stability? How can we reinforce these same behaviors in the classroom? What steps can we take to ensure that our students have opportunities to meaningfully contribute to their own education, just as they meaningfully contribute to the welfare of the home? How can we show real interest in their lives, get inside their quality world, and affirm them as unique individuals? And, finally, how can we provide an emotionally stable environment in the classroom, an environment in which no student will ever feel threatened or suffer loss of dignity?

That's a tall order. It's a tall order for parents with two children, brought up in the same house with the same values, customs, traditions, life styles, and prejudices. It is an even taller order for teachers with twenty-five children, all coming from different households, with a wide variety of values, customs, traditions, life styles, and prejudices. But that is our challenge. So let's take on that challenge and look at how we can mirror in the classroom the same behaviors that we are encouraging parents to mirror in their homes.

Providing Opportunities to Contribute: The Classroom as Cooperative Learning Experience

There is no commitment without involvement: If we want our students to be committed to their responsibilities, we need to involve them in the decisions that result in the determination of those responsibilities. We need, in short, to involve them in the processes through which decisions are made about the classroom, through which classroom problems are solved, and through which classroom housekeeping takes place. In this way, we replicate, as much as possible, the effective home in which children are raised with chores and responsibilities and in which decisions are made with respect for all involved.

The classroom is not a democracy, in which the majority decides every issue. But nor should it be a dictatorship, benevolent or otherwise, in which the teacher makes all decisions. In discussing the social climate of a classroom, like the social climate of a house, I prefer to think of a system characterized by the following:

• a set of principles that stands above all members of the system, students and teachers alike; these would include such things as mutual respect in all interactions, the protection of a learning atmosphere, the insistence that the classroom belongs to all and is the responsibility of all, the higher responsibility of the teacher as the person ultimately responsible and accountable for the successful working of the system, etc.

• a set of guidelines, in the determination of which all members of the system are involved; these would include classroom rules and

278

consequences, chores and responsibilities, etc.

• specific processes for decision making and problem solving; these might include class meetings, collaborative learning activities, etc.

This social climate is more akin to what we call a republic, a system in which certain principles, determined in advance and standing above all that we do, serve as parameters within which decision making and problem solving can take place. It is a system characterized by universal acceptance of the guiding principles, mutual respect for all participants, subsidiarity (the principle that states that the person or group of persons closest to the problem should be the first to be allowed to solve the problem), and collaboration. It is a system our country has been working hard to perfect for over two hundred years now, with high points and low points along the way. It is system worthy of our continuing efforts to perfect, whether in our government, in our homes, or in our classrooms.

How can this work most effectively in the classroom? I offer the following specific recommendations regarding classroom responsibilities and homework, designed to provide an atmosphere that encourages responsibility and success:

• Use class meetings to establish a process within which discussion about classroom responsibilities, housekeeping, conduct, class work, and homework can take place.

• *Do* ensure that every student has some classroom responsibility, at least for some significant part of the school year; this helps communicate to the student that he is important to the group and that he would be missed if he were not present.

• *Do* assign homework on a regular basis; this helps reinforce the habit of doing homework and it communicates that homework is an integral part of schooling.

• *Do* refer to homework in a positive and encouraging way rather than in a manner that communicates drudgery; I like to refer to homework as "opportunities for further enhancement" which, although it doesn't fool your average sixth grader, does nonetheless communicate its purpose more positively . . . and perhaps with a touch of humor.

• *Do* take note of the variety of intelligences and talents when assigning class work and homework, and try to assign work that involves as wide a range of intelligences as possible.

• *Do not* assign homework that demands parent involvement; remember that homework is the student's responsibility, not the parents'. (Like everything else in life, there are exceptions to this. A homework assignment that requires students to ask their parents how life was different when they were growing up, for example, would be an excellent example of an assignment that could appropriately and very effectively involve the parents. But parents should not be expected to be sitting with their children during homework, and we teachers need to ensure that the homework that is assigned is homework that can be done by the student alone.)

Showing Real Interest: Looking for Ways to Affirm Each Child

Margie Stevenson attended a fairly expensive private preparatory school with a reputation for building community among the students and providing a top quality academic education. When her first report card came home, her mother noticed that she was doing quite well- 'A's and 'B's- in all subjects except one, geometry, in which she had a 'D.' The unusually low grade, combined with the fact that Margie had always done well in math, prompted her mother to call the teacher for a conference. After she introduced herself, she asked the teacher if Margie was perhaps not paying attention in class or not doing her homework, given the low grade on the report card. The teacher's reply will not soon be forgotten: "I have no idea why she's doing poorly in my class. In fact, I don't even know who Margie Stevenson is. After all, I've got some six courses to teach with well over 100 students and this is only the first quarter of the school year."

Teaching geometry may very well be a high priority for Margie's teacher, but showing real interest in the students is clearly not. Two months into the school year, this teacher could not even identify one of her students, much less be in a position to get to know her or show interest in her. Whether this is more a commentary on the teacher or on the state of our schools, with their large class sizes and student populations numbering a thousand or more, we don't know. But it is a sad situation either way, and one we must be prepared to overcome.

We teachers must make every effort to get into our students' quality world. We need to know who they are, what their interests are, what their talents are, and what their special needs are. This is not easy to do in the classroom. The typical American home has two children; the typical classroom has well over twenty. That difference alone makes the challenge daunting. But it is essential to make the effort if we are to communicate to our students that they are truly uniquely gifted.

Much is being written today about different learning styles and intelligences. Students are being identified as visual learners or auditory learners, mainstream or special needs, ADHD or 'normal.' Teachers are being encouraged, and sometimes enjoined, to devise individual learning plans for each child, to make modifications in the curriculum for specially identified students, and to teach to each child's particular sensory strength and intelligence. And the sentiment behind all this- the recognition that each child is unique- is a very positive one.

But it is arguable how much the teacher can do to individualize the curriculum to meet each child's needs. In fact, it is arguable whether or not it is even a good idea- does the "real world" individualize itself to meet the needs of each adult? Further, we should not only play to each student's strengths, but also strive to shore up his weaknesses.

But what the teacher *can* do, and what the teacher *must* do, is be sensitive to the fact of differing learning styles and incorporate as many as possible, and as frequently as possible, throughout the curriculum, for the benefit of *all* students. In other words, although we probably cannot adapt each lesson to each different child's learning style, we can create lessons that utilize as many styles as possible and present them in a more creative way to all students. A lesson on the causes of the Civil War that includes textbook readings, teacher presentations, story telling, songs, poetry readings, student presentations, book reports, student-designed projects, a trip to a museum, a live debate on one of the hot issues of the war years, and even the physically acting out of a major battle is certainly more likely to reach all the students than one that relies on just one or two learning modalities. To sum up: Use as many styles as possible in presenting each lesson, thereby maximizing the possibility of each student learning to his fullest potential.

In addition to being sensitive to the plurality of learning styles, there are numerous other ways that we teachers can demonstrate real interest in each child. What follows are several specific ways to communicate to the student that we know that he counts in our classroom:

• One-on-one time- special time set aside with a student to learn about his interests and needs; there may well be no more effective thing we can do to demonstrate real interest in a child than to meet with him one on one.

• Beginning-of-the-year interest inventories- giving the students opportunities to write down their favorite things, their likes and dislikes, subjects they'd like to learn more about, etc., gives the teacher ideas for special projects and emphases, as well as the opportunity to learn more about the children individually.

• Student-of-the-week- giving the students opportunities to take "center stage," if only for a day or week, allows them to share their interests with the class, and allows the class to individually affirm each student.

- Portfolios- this welcome addition to student assessment allows the student to participate in her own evaluation by giving examples of things that *she* feels are significant, rather than just what the teacher feels are significant; in addition, it provides an excellent opportunity for one-on-one attention as the student explains the items in her portfolio with the teacher.

- Personal notes- special notes to children on birthdays, special occasions, or for no reason at all communicate to the child that you are thinking about him.

- Cooperative learning activities- although the teacher may not learn more about each child during cooperative learning activities, the students will, and they will be given the opportunity to demonstrate otherwise untapped abilities such as group problem solving, peer tutoring, resourcefulness, and cooperation, to name just a few.

It has been said that the best predictor of a child's success in the classroom is his perception of whether or not the teacher likes him. Make the effort to show each child in the class that you truly do like him by showing real interest in his interests and abilities.

Providing Emotional Stability: The Classroom as Safe Haven

Madeline. Hunter is remembered most for her work on the lesson cycle and the various elements that comprise the effective lesson, from stating the objective to closure. Unfortunately, many school districts took her insights to mean that every lesson must contain every element of the classic lesson cycle, even though Hunter made it clear that that was not the case. But such is the fate of prophets: Their disciples often betray them, though unwittingly.

What Hunter made clear is that although all these elements are important aspects of the effective lesson, they need not be present in *every* lesson. In fact, she declares quite forcefully that in teaching, everything is relative and situational, and the effective teacher must read the situation and choose which elements of the cycle are appropriate, at this time and with these students, and which are not appropriate. That is the art of teaching.

But Hunter does not stop by saying that everything in teaching is relative and situational. She throws in an exception, one critical to our understanding of providing emotional stability in the classroom. In teaching, she says, everything is relative and situational except one thing: We must never cause a child to lose dignity.

We must never cause a child to lose dignity. In the words we use, the tone of voice we project, the attitude we display, we must never communicate to the student that he is unworthy of dignity and respect. Very few of us would ever do that intentionally-thankfully, sarcasm and demeaning words and phrases have long since gone into disfavor in the classroom-, but there are many ways that we might do so without realizing it. To pick just one example, how long do we wait for a child to respond after we ask a question? Research has shown that that is very much dependent upon our perception of the child- if we perceive the child as bright, we will wait longer; if we perceive her as not-so-bright we will more quickly go on to another student. But does that communicate dignity and respect for the less-bright student?

Let us always be vigilant, even over-scrupulous, in our efforts to ensure that every interaction we have with a child in the classroom be one that upholds her dignity and respect. If they learn nothing else from us, let them at least learn that they are persons of dignity, something that will carry over and hopefully be reinforced in the home, in the community, and, later, on the job.

Walking the Talk: Being A Model for the Children

It bears repeating one more time: We cannot change others; we can only change ourselves. But in doing so we provide a model, an incentive, an opportunity for others to change. In that spirit, what behaviors must *we* project if we want our students to further their development as capable, respectful, and responsible children? The following chart will use the same twelve behaviors recommended for parents with their children in our chapter on role modeling and suggest ways that we can support those behaviors in the classroom:

Behaviors We Want Our Students to Learn	**Behaviors We Must Then Demonstrate**
1. To be on time for class	To model the importance of being on time for class, *we* must be on time for class; in fact, let's be *early* for class, to demonstrate how important it is to be prepared
2. To enjoy reading	Read to your students; tell them about enjoyable books you have read;

encourage them to talk about their favorite books; make book reports more enjoyable by giving options for format (written, oral, illustrated, performed, etc.); display quality works of literature in the classroom

3. To avoid excessive TV — Talk about games and activities you enjoyed when you were younger; avoid using the classroom to talk about the previous night's TV shows; avoid careless references to "junk" TV shows; occasionally recommend quality specials to demonstrate discriminating use of TV

4. To be positive about their school — Always act like you enjoy being here; be "upbeat" about your school; project positive expectations about the students' progress and possibilities

5. To be interested in what is going on in the school — Talk about the various school activities; highlight them on your bulletin board; invite the students to share their school activities with the class; attend the various school activities

6. To be problem solvers	Avoid trying to solve all the students' problems; emphasize problem solving rather than blaming; throw the problems back to the students with statements such as: "I can see how that would be a problem. Why don't we all try to solve it. You all offer possible solutions and I will write them on the board, and then we will choose the best"; use class meetings to encourage them to solve problems
7. To be respectful	*Always, always, always* treat the children with respect; remember: "There is only one absolute in teaching and that is that we must never cause a child to lose dignity"; if the temptation arises to respond to a child disrespectfully, model "time out" by putting off the conversation until you have calmed down
8. To respect the teaching profession	Model all these behaviors and your students will respect the teaching profession . . . and you!
9. To participate in classroom chores and responsibilities	Avoid using clean-up time to catch up on lesson plans or other work; instead, model the spirit of

	cooperation and the dignity of manual work by doing chores yourself during clean-up time
10. To be good listeners	Avoid interrupting; follow the ten-second rule when asking a question (wait ten seconds after asking one student a question before going on to another student); reflect back to the student what he has said
11. To develop healthy attitudes about marriage and sexuality	Tell the students stories about your spouse or your parents that demonstrate positive attitudes about married life
12. To be spiritual persons	Separation of church and state does not mean the exclusion of the spiritual from daily life- do not hesitate to talk about your own spirituality; communicate respect for the many ways of being spiritual persons; give explanations for actions that communicate a higher power or a natural law (for example, say "because it's the right thing to do" rather than "because I said so")

Clearly, much is expected of us educators. And that's the way it should be. After all, there is no higher profession than that which develops the potentials of the future leadership of our world. We cannot afford to be anything but the very best we can be.

POSTSCRIPT

LOOKING FORWARD

Never look back;
they might be gaining on you.

-Satchel Paige

I have thought often of those students who entered my frame of reference those seven days in April several years back, occasioning a change in life direction for me. The mom who left her husband and visited me to ask that I keep an eye on her daughter has been back and forth with him several times since then. She appears to be caught up in a codependent relationship, both with her husband and with her daughter, who needs continuous affirmation at school.

The sixteen-year-old who ran away from home eventually dropped out of school, got into difficulties with alcohol, and is now struggling to hold down a job. Teddy, the would-be stalker, has yet to learn effective communication skills and is becoming more and more alienated from his fellow students, and from his parents, daily. Joanna, the girl who regularly came to school with wads of money, is now heavily involved in an ethnic gang. As for the three abuse calls, although we still get them on a regular basis, I have not since received three in a seven-day period. And I have not had any calls regarding those same three children. So I guess that's progress.

291

But more importantly, the process of providing opportunities for parents and teachers to review and improve their skills is now very much in place in our community. We now have a process in place for parents who are experiencing difficulty in their relationships, and those who are not yet experiencing any significant difficulties, to come together and learn from each other. Those seven days in April have never since been repeated, nothing even close, and I attribute it with confidence to the introduction of the Developing Capable People program in our school community. The needs of the Teddys and Joannas and Marias and Richards, and their parents, are more effectively being met.

As of this writing, I have facilitated some twenty-five Developing Capable People courses, the nine-week program designed by H. Stephen Glenn to increase the quality of life in families, schools, and organizations. Those twenty-five courses have involved some 300 parents, including many teachers. In addition, I have trained well over 100 counselors, teachers, principals, youth ministers, and parent leaders to facilitate the courses themselves and take them to their respective communities. As a result, the programs are presently being offered in schools, churches, and community centers throughout the Dallas area and beyond, reaching thousands more. And there are facilitators all over the country, indeed in many parts of the world, doing the same. The world is being changed, one person at a time.

On a more personal note, I have been reconfirmed in my role as educator and school principal. There are still moments of despair- especially during April!- but I now have a response to that despair. I can fall back on the many experiences I have had working with parents, providing opportunities for them to make positive changes in their lives, learning from them so that I too could make positive changes in my own life. I now have a process for change, and it is a liberating and empowering feeling.

In reading this book, you have become part of that change, that process of reviewing and improving your own skills. You have reflected upon the stories presented, applied them to your own lives, and, no doubt, made mental notes on what changes you would like to make in the future. Let's now close this book with the invitation to jot down those thoughts, thereby participating in that very important exercise of formalizing our commitments by putting them in writing.

So I ask you to reflect now on each of the three behaviors we have looked at. What things have you identified that you would like to do differently? What specific changes would you like to make? What behaviors would you like to more effectively model for your children? And how, specifically, will you make these changes?

Write down your thoughts on the "Personal Commitment Page" that follows. Commit yourself to them. Make them your own. And confirm it all with your signature.

It has been said that the healing of a nation begins in the homes of its citizens. I would add that the healing of what may be wrong with our schools also begins in our homes. Let's begin that healing- for us, for our children, and for future generations of Americans- by striving to provide in our own homes an environment characterized by Contribution, Affirmation, and Emotional Stability.

MY PERSONAL COMMITMENT PAGE

In order to maximize the potential for my children to experience success and happiness in school, I will make the following specific changes in my life:

Contribution: Organizing My Family for Household Chores

Affirmation: Showing Real Interest in My Children's Interests

Emotional Stability: Providing an Oasis in My Home

_____   _____

(signature)   (date)

FOR MORE INFORMATION

For more information regarding presentations or seminars, contact:

Mike Brock
Building Community
P. O. Box 810483
Farmers Branch TX 75381

telephone: (972) 243-7105, extension 10

fax: (972) 484-6187

Michael L. Brock is a school principal in the Dallas, Texas, area and founder and director of *Building Community,* through which he offers presentations, workshops, seminars, and leadership training. *School-Smart Parenting: Raising Children for Success and Happiness in School* is the result of insights developed during his 25 years in education working with literally thousands of students and their families, as well as his own experiences sharing in the raising of his two children, Thomas and Jennifer. Carol, his wife of 27 years, teaches kindergarten.

Mike has spoken to national audiences in New York, Chicago, New Orleans, and Toronto, and has given numerous workshops and presentations throughout Texas. In addition to being the title of his book, *School-Smart Parenting: Raising Children for Success and Happiness in School* is also the title of his most frequently requested presentation and workshop.